TIME OUT!

A SPORTS FAN'S DREAM YEAR

TIME OUT!
A SPORTS FAN'S DREAM YEAR

EDGAR WELDEN
As Told To
KEITH DUNNAVANT

WILL Publishing
LLC.
BIRMINGHAM • ALABAMA

TIME OUT!
A SPORTS FAN'S DREAM YEAR

Edgar Welden / Keith Dunnavant

ISBN: 0-9668486-0-8

Library of Congress Catalog Card Number: 98-061810

Book Design by J. Durham Design
Cover Jacket Design By J. Durham Design
Cover Photograph by Mark L. Wright

First Edition 1999

Printed in the U.S.A.

DEDICATION

To my mother, Dot,

for passing on to me her

personality and her love and

passion for going and doing.

•

To my daughter, Ann,

who has inherited her joy

of travel and adventurous spirit

from Dot and me.

•

To my wife, Louise,

who must be a saint

for putting up with

all my foolishness.

You are very special.

TIME OUT!

A SPORTS FAN'S DREAM YEAR

TABLE OF CONTENTS

ACKNOWLEDGMENTS

THE TRIP, THANKS TO:

Mercedes Marbach, Wolf Camera, sold me my camera, processed my hundreds of rolls of film and was always helpful and accommodating.

Joni Carper, Golden Tickets, was prompt and professional while making it possible for me to have good tickets, often on short notice.

Guylene Jackson and her staff at GO Travel dealt with continuing changes without hanging up on me.

John and **Caroline Abele, Fletcher Abele** and **Borden Burr** and the staff at All Seasons Travel probably reached the point that they didn't want to hear my voice, due to my schedule changes as my calendar reacted to wins and losses.

Clay Manley, David Neill and **David Browder** all helped do research, investigate schedules and track down detailed information for events.

John McMahon is a true friend and made some extremely difficult tickets available and events possible.

THE BOOK, THANKS TO:

Jake Reiss was the first person to encourage me to write a book and share my story.

James Powell and **Emily Herring** helped me with research.

Charlie Stewart, a longtime friend, continued talking to folks about my book needing a good title, until someone really listened, and **Alex O. Gatewood,** a mutual friend from Tuscaloosa, came up with the title "Time Out!".

John Clements, a close friend, has given me constant encouragement, direction and guidance.

SPECIAL THANKS

Due to life's complications and responsibilities, any commitment that you make must have an understanding and supportive cast — Chasing your dream is no different. Naturally, it starts with your entire family. All of my family made sacrifices and adjustments around my schedule. In addition, thankfully, everyone remained in good health throughout my travel year. I thank all of my family.

The fulfillment of this dream would not have been possible without the complete support of my business partners: my brother Charles Welden and his sons Chuck and Bill Welden, Pete Field and his son Robert Field, and my son Ed Welden. A special thanks to each of you.

In addition to my partners, I want to thank, from the bottom of my heart, our dedicated fellow workers who keep the businesses going.

I can't say enough about my loyal assistant, Karen Pierce. Karen is dependable, helpful, hardworking, competent and ever-cheerful. During my travel year, she helped me take care of my daily business responsibilities. I don't know why she puts up with me — but — I couldn't do without her. Thanks, Karen.

My daughter Ann researched events, scheduled and rescheduled airline tickets, hotel reservations and car rentals. She secured tickets, helped plan my trip and worked hard to make it as worry-free as possible. Ann kept my calendar and maintained my daily event files throughout the year by organizing ticket stubs, programs, newspaper articles, photographs, etc. for each trip. Ann kept me informed of events as they changed and truly stayed on top of things. Thanks for your tireless energy.

Thanks to my son Ed and his wife Danielle for giving Louise and me our first grandson, Will. And thanks to Will for providing me a publisher for my book.

And Keith Dunnavant, my partner in writing, was a natural for this book. Like me, Keith also grew up in a small Alabama town and attended the University of Alabama. He is a big sports fan and has vast knowledge due to his national sports press experience. I enjoyed working with Keith and appreciate his patience and hard work.

Last but not least, my special thanks to Mary Gantt, the person most responsible for pressing forward and pulling together the hundreds of details necessary to get this book from an idea to the reality of it appearing on bookstore shelves.

Chasing the Dream

Have you ever wanted to just run away? As kids, I guess we all do. It's human nature. All of us naturally want to run away from our ordinary lives and have some great adventure. That's what this book is all about. It took me 40 years to convince myself to run away and chase my dream.

I was born in 1943 and grew up in the small town of Wetumpka, Alabama. I was a typical kid, which is to say, I always loved sports. Wetumpka, the county seat of Elmore County, located about 15 miles north of Montgomery in the central part of the state, had a population in those days of about 4,000 people. The Coosa River flows through the center of town, with a beautiful old arched bridge separating the business district from the residential sections. It was your average small Southern town, where everybody knew everybody. People left their doors unlocked. It was a wonderful place to grow up with my older brother Charles and younger sister Vicki. My daddy, Vic Welden, owned a full-service grocery store in the middle of the business district, and that's where Charles and I worked on many Saturdays to make spending money. My mother, Dot, was the bookkeeper for the operation.

My introduction to the business world came in the years following World War II when I would ride along with my uncle, William Harris, on what was known then as the rolling store, an extension of Vic's Supermarket. Daddy had two to four rolling stores operating at any given time. The rolling stores consisted of truck cabs with rear ends resembling school buses, filled with shelves that were stocked with grocery items. The trucks would load up at Vic's Supermarket early in the morning and head off in different directions to rural parts of the county, where many people had no way to get into town to buy sugar, flour, meal, and canned goods. Ours was not a strictly cash-and-carry business. Often we would barter with our customers, sometimes trading a pound of coffee or some other staple for a dozen eggs or a sack full of home-grown tomatoes.

My father was extremely supportive of his children, whether in sports or anything else. He was a loving father who taught us many things, including the value of a good work ethic, how special customers are, and never to quit. These are qualities Charles and I have endeavored to stress in our business and pass on to our children. Our success in business is directly linked to the values taught to us by our father, who passed away in 1991. In addition to teaching us how to keep a set of books, my mother was involved with all aspects of her children's activities and continues to teach us to this day the importance of family.

My brother Charles, who was four grades ahead of me in school, has always been as supportive a big brother as anyone ever had. Just recently, I saw for the first time a postcard Daddy sent to Charles during World War II while he was stationed in the south of France. The postcard, dated June 20, 1945, commended Charles for being such a "big boy" for having his tonsils removed. At the time, Charles and I were sharing a room in the Wetumpka General Hospital where we both had tonsillectomies. I also had a little additional surgery — I was circumcised. Charles tells the story of friends coming to visit and asking about our surgery. Charles would say, "Edgar, show them your surgery," and I would pull down my pants. The last sentence of the postcard reads, "Take care of Edgar." He always has.

My sister Vicki, who was six grades behind me in school, has always been the darling of the family. Daddy had his own brand of flour that he sold at the grocery store — "Vic's Pride." The sack featured a picture of Vicki in her Sunday best. She is a wonderful mother and an outstanding schoolteacher. She and her husband Doug, a CPA, have raised two great kids, Monty and Leigh.

Sports occupied an awful lot of my time. If the truth be known, my family often accused me of using sports to get out of working at the grocery store. We lived a block from the recreation center and four blocks from the school's athletic facilities, and in those days, we didn't specialize in particular sports. There were only so many of us boys and we pretty much played everything, although I was probably better at tennis and basketball than anything else. After my high school senior year, in 1961, I was honored to be selected from our region to play in the Alabama North-South All-Star basketball game at Foster Auditorium on the University of Alabama campus. It was a great experience, playing on the same floor as the famed Rocket Eight teams of the '50s, but I didn't see much action.

Some of my friends in Birmingham, after years of listening to me bellow on about Wetumpka and our football prowess, tease me about holding the state record for the longest pass play that failed to score a touchdown. They might be right. When I was in the 10th grade, Wetumpka was playing Union Springs. I was the second-string quarterback and Union Springs had us backed up to the one-inch line. We were all worried about giving up a safety.

The coach grabbed me on the sideline and said, "Go in there and throw 80 pass!" Well, 80 pass was where you fake it to the fullback up the middle, drop back and throw it to the end running down the middle of the field. Back then we didn't have four wide-outs and three flankers like Steve Spurrier's teams do now. All we had was a right end and a left end, so it didn't take a rocket scientist to figure out your passing routes.

I called the play, faked to the fullback and threw a pass down the middle. The end caught it, ran a long way and was tackled just short of the goal line. We had a 99-yard play that didn't score. This has to be a record. Now, you know how these football stories get exaggerated as they're retold time after time through the years. Maybe he got tackled on the 10 yard-line. Truth is, I don't remember for sure.

Of course, in those days, most schools only competed in football, basketball, baseball and track. I loved tennis, so my junior year in high school, I got together with my friends Tommy Stowe and Willie Watson and we started a tennis team. That probably sounds a little odd nowadays, when having a tennis team is so common for high schools. But then it was rare for small schools.

There were so few tennis teams in Alabama in those days, I think all you had to do was show up to play in the state tournament. So we headed off to Sylacauga, the three of us who just decided to start our own tennis team. We looked in the paper to find out that the doubles team Wetumpka was facing, Ed Hatch and Donald Sweeney, had won the state tournament the previous two years! So naturally, they drilled us, 6-0, 6-0. But we loved it, anyway, because we were competing and having fun.

In those days, before around-the-clock sports coverage on television, if you lived in a small town like Wetumpka, your exposure to the outside sports world was pretty limited. I had a real thirst for sports. Many years we asked for tickets and went to the Blue-Gray all-star football game at Cramton Bowl in Montgomery. That was a big deal. I was an Auburn football fan in those days, and Shug Jordan had the Tigers on top, and on many occasions, we would make the hour's drive to Auburn to see them play. I remember going to the Garrett Coliseum in Montgomery the night Alabama beat Kentucky in basketball with the Rocket Eight in 1956. Man, what a thrill. I mean, to beat Kentucky in those days! Nobody in the SEC could touch Adolph Rupp's team. One of my fondest memories from those years was going to Garrett Coliseum to see Poncho Gonzales and his fellow pros put on a tennis exhibition.

At that time, television whet your appetite for sports but the coverage was mostly confined to the big events. I loved to watch the Major League Baseball Game-of-the-Week, the college bowl games, the U.S. Open tennis tournament, Gillette's Friday Night Fights, and other stuff like that, imagining what it would be like to go to those far-away places and actually attend sporting events. This was a dream that captivated me from a very early age.

After graduating from high school in 1961, I decided to attend the University of Alabama, and, of course, Paul "Bear" Bryant's dynasty was just hitting its stride. I pledged KA and got involved in the fraternity scene and just had a lot of fun. Turns out, my four years were the same four years as a guy named Joe Namath. It was a big deal for us to get a date and go to the football games in Birmingham, but none of us ever had much money, so we would go down to Druid City Hospital and sell a pint of blood for $15 in order to finance our weekend partying!

In the years after I graduated from college, I continued to be a big sports fan, but naturally, it took a backseat as I started building a career and a family. About the time I finished college, I got involved in Republican Party politics in Alabama, which led me to become state chairman in 1975. In 1987, I spent a year heading up the economic development effort for the State of Alabama under the administration of Governor Guy Hunt, who was our first Republican governor since Reconstruction. Throughout most of the last 30 years, however, my "day job" has been in the private sector. Upon graduation from college in 1965, Charles and I, with the support and guidance of our parents, started in the convenience store business.

We had participated in the transition from the rolling store to the full-service grocery store to some of the first convenience stores in the state of Alabama with self-service gas, which was one of the biggest changes in the retail business over the last three decades. In 1977, I joined Charles and Pete Field as a partner in several business ventures which continue to this day.

Like all Birmingham sports fans, I have watched the city win and lose several sports franchises over the last three decades. In the early '90s, when the World League of American Football was formed, I was able to combine my love of sports and business to become a minority owner in the Birmingham Fire. We all had a lot of fun, but in the end, the Fire became the latest of the Magic City's doomed franchises, even though we produced the future head coach of the Dallas Cowboys, Chan Gailey.

Through the years, I often took sports trips with my wife Louise and our children Ed and Ann. Sometimes we planned in advance, sometimes not. They still kid me about our trip to the 1984 Olympics in Los Angeles. I was sitting at home one night watching the wrestling competition on television and got really interested in the story of this wrestler who had been seriously ill but overcame his illness to win a medal. And I just said to myself, "I need to be out there."

Right then, I called our friend and travel agent, Grantland Rice, and told him I wanted to leave the next day to go to the Olympics. Just like that. I didn't have any tickets, no place to stay. My son was a teenager at the time and I told him to be ready to leave early the next morning; we were going somewhere fun. I wouldn't tell him where.

So the next day, we got on the plane and went to L.A. We had great seats to watch the USA play France in basketball. We sat right behind the bench. Bobby Knight was coaching and it was an amazing team, probably the best college team they ever had in the Olympics. Michael Jordan. Wayman Tisdale. Patrick Ewing.

Well, turns out we were supposed to be having dinner with our friends, the Stewarts, at the beach and had forgotten to tell them we had flown to California on the spur of the moment. As they were watching the basketball game on television, wondering where we were, the camera went to a crowd shot and their son Jay yelled, "Y'all look! There's Edgar!" That's when they figured out we weren't coming for dinner.

About a decade later, I started thinking about all those dreams I'd had as a child, about seeing all those great sporting events in one great adventurous trip. The trip would be as much for the experience of the travel as for the events themselves.

One of the things that inspired me was a trip that an old friend of mine from Demopolis, Jim Rogers, had taken. If any of you watch the financial news on television, you've probably seen Jim being grilled for expert analysis on the stock market. He's a retired New York investment banker who always wears a bow tie. Several years ago, he took a year off and traveled the world with his girlfriend on his motorcycle. What came out of his experience was this wonderful book, *Investment Biker*, in which he talks about his sojourn across the globe.

Well, I thought it might be interesting to take that idea and apply it to sports, a sports-themed world tour. Go to all the great sporting events and see the world at the same time. So in 1995, I hired a young man who had recently graduated from Vanderbilt, Clay Manley, to research all the big events across the globe and see if it was a feasible idea. In short, it wasn't. We decided it would have been a logistical nightmare to make all the big events worldwide, because I would have to be constantly crisscrossing the globe.

I decided to narrow my focus. Instead of a world tour, I would go on an American sporting adventure and experience as many events as possible (and, as an added bonus, fulfill the desire to visit all 50 state capitols). Because of my involvement with the Republican Party, I decided to skip 1996, which was a national election year, and put the trip off until 1997. (In 1996, I was elected Republican National Committeeman for the state of Alabama, which meant I would be involved in numerous party functions throughout the year. But I figured I could schedule most of my tour around these commitments). Even toward the end of 1996, however, when all the plans were in place, I was still afraid that something would interfere at the last minute.

Right before Christmas, 1996, the whole family went to the Cayman Islands for vacation, one last family gathering before I started my tour. While we were in the Caymans, my daughter Ann accepted Jamie Holman's marriage proposal. Jamie grew up in Dothan and was Ed's little brother in Sigma Nu at the University of Alabama, where he and Ann met. Louise and I were pleased with Ann's choice for many reasons. Not only is Jamie a good kid, but he had played quarterback at Northview High in Dothan, which gave him some credibility with me. They decided the wedding would be the following May, which could have complicated matters. But they assured me we could plan around it, and they wanted me to take the trip (probably to get me out of their hair!).

At first, when I started talking about my dream, my wife played along in a condescending way. It wasn't real to her. During 1995 and '96, when I started seriously planning the trip, she was not encouraging. No wife wants her spouse to go off for a whole year. But eventually, when she realized I was serious and how much the trip meant to me, Louise became supportive. I encouraged Louise to go with me to as many events as she wanted, and she accompanied me on numerous trips. More than that, however, she allowed me to pursue my dream with her blessing, and I cannot say how much I love her and appreciate her for putting up with me.

At the end of 1996, the recent deaths of two very special people whom I was fortunate to call friends, Ronnie Noojin and Frank Nix, were weighing heavily on my mind. Both men were about my age and were big sports fans. The combined effect of their deaths was pretty staggering for a guy who's spent most of his life working while deferring his dream for someday. Well, what if "someday" never came? What if I were lucky enough to live to be 75 years old but then looked back on all the things I had not done? Life is short and who knows when your time is up?

The more I thought about it, I didn't want to be a guy who looked back on his life and wondered what might have been. (A month into the trip, these thoughts would be reinforced when my good friend Jamie Rainer, who is my age, was in apparent good health one day and forced to undergo heart bypass surgery the next. Jamie would recover, but his ordeal scared me into having a stress test and gave me even greater motivation to complete my trip.)

So right after Christmas, Louise accompanied me as I embarked on my year on the road. Although I would return home every week or so, I would spend the vast majority of 1997 living out of my suitcase. Even now, looking back, the numbers seem staggering to me: Over one 12-month period, I attended 250 sporting events, traveling 109,659 miles by air, 10,178 miles by land, spending 204 nights in hotels and visiting 131 different cities.

I saw Mike Tyson take a bite out of Evander Holyfield's ear. I saw a game in every Major League Baseball ballpark. I rode a dog sled at The Iditarod. I saw Dean Smith break Adolph Rupp's record for college basketball victories and I saw the first interleague baseball game. I saw all the blockbuster showdowns including the Super Bowl, the World Series and the NBA Finals, and also less-publicized events such as the X-Games, the World Nine-Ball Championships and a lumberjack contest.

But it was more than a year of sporting events. It was the most incredible adventure of my life. ■

CHAPTER ONE

Roses, Sugar and Jim Beam

D uring Governor Guy Hunt's administration, I worked on his
staff basically as a volunteer special assistant, but for liability
purposes, they paid me $1 per pay period. My friends often ribbed me
about being the $1 a week man. After taxes, I think it amounted to
about 60 cents. I still have the checks. You know what people say:
You get what you pay for.

But there were fringe benefits to the job, and one of them was
being appointed by the governor to the board of the Alabama
Music Hall of Fame in Tuscumbia. Alabama is proud to claim
many wonderful artists as her sons and daughters: Toni Tenille,
Lionel Ritchie, Jim Nabors, Tammy Wynette, Hank Williams,
Sr., Hank Williams, Jr., Emmy Lou Harris, Nat King Cole, and
the well-known group Alabama, to name a few.

Every other year, the Hall of Fame has a big induction banquet in Huntsville. In addition to the new inductees, various
other artists with Alabama ties usually perform, making it one of
the most important musical events in the state. In 1995, the legendary Percy Sledge, who had been inducted several years
before, was scheduled to be one of the featured singers. Even

though Percy has been out of the spotlight for years, his 1960s hit, "When a Man Loves a Woman," remains a classic and a real crowd-pleaser anytime he takes the stage.

On the night of the banquet, Louise and I and three other couples — Boots and Louise Gale, John and Betty McMahon and Frank and Karle Falkenburg — hired a van to drive us from Birmingham to the ceremonies in Huntsville. Since I was on the board, everyone was quizzing me about who was going to be there that night, and the one that captured everyone's attention was Percy Sledge. Well, the more wine we drank, the closer buddies Percy and I became! Oh, yeah, I would say, Percy and I go way back! We're tight! I was just having a little fun. But of course, Percy Sledge didn't know who the hell I was.

So when the van pulled up to the Von Braun Civic Center we all got out and were feeling pretty good. And who came walking by? You guessed it. Percy Sledge. He was walking along toward the stage door with a woman on each arm. Well, I couldn't let on that I didn't know the guy, so I decided to see if I could carry the bit a little farther. I yelled out, "Percy, my main man!" And he stopped in his tracks.

I guess he thought he was supposed to have known me from somewhere, because he came up to me and gave me a big hug and acted like he was my best friend. I introduced him to all the folks and we made pictures. All the while, he had no idea who I was. But all my friends were impressed.

Later that night, when we were riding home after watching Percy and the other stars put on a fantastic show, I told everybody that if my daughter Ann ever got married, I would get my buddy

Percy to come sing "When a Man Loves a Woman" at her wedding reception. I never expected them to remember my pledge.

The first week of my trip would be dominated by the college bowl games and the NFL playoffs. Those are the kinds of events we had planned months in advance. But as often would be the case throughout the year, the opening week included several doses of improvisation. Working with my travel agents, and my daughter Ann, who arranged most of my travel, I often added or subtracted events at the last minute.

On the day after Christmas, Thursday, December 26, 1996, Louise and I got up at 4:30 in the morning to catch a 6 a.m. Delta flight to Sacramento. This had already been an unusual Christmas for us. It was the first time since our children were born that we had spent Christmas Eve and Christmas Day alone. Our son, 27-year-old Ed, was with his wife Danielle, visiting her family in Livingston. Our 24-year-old daughter Ann was with her fiancé Jamie Holman, visiting his family in Dothan. They all returned to our home on Christmas Night for dinner and to open our family presents. They were also anxious to see if their mother had talked their daddy into calling off his foolish trip.

When we got to the ticket counter at the Birmingham International Airport, I put on my Alabama hat and made Louise hold up the line to make a picture of me departing on my grand adventure. You could see that Louise, who was going with me on this leg, was embarrassed. I'm sure some of those people behind us in line must have thought that this yokel in the Kentucky basketball warm-up suit wanted to record his very first airplane trip.

I had planned to start my trip with the Rose Bowl, the so-called Granddaddy of Them All. But after checking the schedules, I decided to go out to California a couple days early to catch an NBA basketball game between Sacramento and Vancouver. Roy Rogers, who had been one of the star players at Alabama the previous year, was a rookie for Vancouver. I had seen Roy at a function earlier in the year and he had encouraged me to contact him if I was able to see one of his NBA games. So through a mutual friend, Ron Edwards, Roy provided us with some good tickets and we were able to catch his game.

When we got to Sacramento, we checked into the Hyatt Regency, where the Vancouver team was staying. We met Roy and some of his teammates in the lobby and they were kind enough to make pictures with us before boarding the team bus to the Arco Arena. Roy played 16 minutes and scored 16 points, but Vancouver lost a close game.

Friday morning, Louise and I decided to tour the California state capitol, which was only a block down the street from our hotel. It was an overcast morning and as we walked up the steps to the capitol, we discovered that we were the only two patrons on the early morning guided tour.

"I can't believe there's only two of us on the tour," I said casually to Louise.

She gave me a funny look. "Edgar, if it had been raining when we left the hotel, there would have only been one person on the tour!"

Because of my love of politics and history, one of the goals of my year on the road was to visit all 50 state capitols. California would be my first, and over the next 12 months, I would go to great lengths to squeeze these sight-seeing side trips into my sports fantasy tour.

After we toured the capitol, we drove from Sacramento to Santa Clara to see the University of Alabama basketball team participate in the Cable Car Classic. At this point in the season, the Crimson Tide was 10-0 and ranked 19th in the nation. It looked like 'Bama was on its way to a fine season, but this tournament would turn the season sour. Alabama lost both games in the tournament at San Jose Arena — close games on consecutive nights to San Jose State and Santa Clara. These games started the downward spiral of Alabama basketball for that season and the next.

A pleasant part of this trip was running into our friends from Birmingham, John and Caroline Abele, who were also there to see the Crimson Tide play. There may not be two more avid 'Bama basketball supporters than John and Caroline. With them were their two grown sons, Fletcher and Chris, and Chris' future wife, Leah. Fletcher was in the travel business with his parents. Fletcher and Chris were really interested in my trip, so they started brainstorming about what events I should attend. Fletcher ended up being very helpful and working out travel arrangements for several of my trips.

Saturday, before the second night of the Cable Car Classic, I realized that the Philadelphia Eagles were playing in San Francisco against the 49ers in the first round of the NFL playoffs the following day. I got on the phone and found a ticket broker and had two tickets overnighted to us at our hotel outside San Francisco, where we would be arriving the next day. Sunday morning we drove from Santa Clara to Lafayette, a suburban community east of San Francisco.

But there was a bad storm moving in; 60-miles-per-hour winds were predicted. It was so bad that the people at The Lafayette Park Hotel cautioned us about trying to cross the Bay Bridge to get to the game, so we changed plans again.

It was a very quaint, beautiful little hotel. We even had a fireplace in our room. I went down to the lobby and gave our two tickets to a bellman and a desk clerk and they scrambled to get off from work to make it to the game. I grabbed a bottle of wine and retreated to our room, where Louise and I watched the 49ers win a big victory in front of a roaring fire, which earned me some brownie points with Louise.

It was a big thrill for those two young men to get to see that game. Playoff tickets for the 49ers are tough to come by, and they couldn't believe I would come all that way to see the game and pass up the opportunity to see it in person. They also couldn't believe I was willing to give the tickets away. They thought I was crazy, which would be a recurring theme with many of the people I would meet throughout the year. San Francisco defeated Philadelphia and advanced to the next round to play at Green Bay and I was determined not to miss that one, regardless of the weather.

The reason we had stayed in that area was because we had three sets of friends who lived east of San Francisco and we had arranged to have dinner with them that night: Peggy Hatley, who had been a friend of mine in college, and her husband Gerald; Jim Clark, who had lived across the street from us in Birmingham; and Sandy Bell, who had been a childhood friend of Louise's, and her husband Ford. We met at Bridges in Danville, which is the restaurant where a memorable scene in the Robin Williams movie "Mrs. Doubtfire" was filmed.

The next morning, we drove to Oakland and flew to Los Angeles and checked into the Beverly Hilton in Beverly Hills, which was full of Ohio State fans there for the upcoming Rose Bowl against Arizona State. Tuesday was a relaxing day spent mostly on Rodeo Drive. I canceled some plans to tour the movie studios and took Louise shopping instead, which ended up being my second good decision of the week. There would come a time when I would need the goodwill I was storing up with Louise.

Wednesday morning, January 1, we got up at 4:30 in the morning to beat the traffic and get a good parking place for the Tournament of Roses Parade. Although we had reserved seats for the parade, which begins at 8 a.m., many people go out the night before and party along the parade route all night long, staking out their positions for the big event.

The traffic around Pasadena was unbelievable, but I must say, the parade was everything we expected it to be. The parade began with a low-flying pass down Colorado Boulevard by a stealth bomber, so called because of its ability to fly undetected by radar. This was the U.S. Air Force's 50th anniversary salute to itself. The Grand Marshals for this 108th Tournament of Roses Parade were U.S. Olympic gold medalists Carl Lewis and Shannon Miller. It's a real hassle getting there and getting out, but I'm glad we got to see it. All those floats! What an incredible show.

A few facts about the Rose Bowl Parade: An estimated 425 million television viewers in more than 100 countries see it each year . . . An estimated 1 million spectators line the 5 1/2 mile-long parade route . . . The average float in the parade contains more floral material than many florists use in five years.

While the parade was going on, Alabama was playing Michigan in the Outback Bowl in Tampa, three hours ahead of us, which was Gene Stallings' final game as the Crimson Tide's head coach. I had my portable telephone with me, so about every 15 minutes, I would call home to check the score. The people sitting next to me were from Alabama and were as interested in the game as I was. 'Bama sent Stallings out a winner — which not only made us Alabama folks happy but also warmed the hearts of all the Ohio State fans at the Rose Bowl, since Michigan is their biggest rival and had knocked the Buckeyes out of the national championship race. We then started making our way over to the mammoth 100,000 seat Rose Bowl, which is one of those almost mythical places I had dreamed about seeing my entire life.

The Rose Bowl pitted No. 2 ranked Arizona State against No. 4 Ohio State, and the Sugar Bowl, which would be played the following night, was between No. 1 Florida State and No. 3 Florida. Both were billing themselves as the showdown for the 1996 national championship. Ohio State had been undefeated all season until falling to Michigan in its regular season finale. Arizona State, which was undefeated, now had a chance to win at least a share of its first national title if it could knock off the Buckeyes.

But even if Arizona State won to lay claim to part of the title, Florida State also was unbeaten and had a chance to say something about the matter in the Sugar Bowl.

The mystique of the Rose Bowl is unmatched in college football. I remember as a youth hearing about all those great Alabama teams of Wallace Wade and Frank Thomas that played in Pasadena, before the game was closed to all but the champions of the Big Ten and Pac-10 right after World War II. I've always wished 'Bama could go back to the Rose Bowl in my lifetime. But frankly, my first visit to the Rose Bowl was a bit of a letdown. I was disappointed by the facility, especially the old bleacher seats, which are too close together, and the poor bathroom and concession facilities. It was a very uncomfortable place to see a game, which would have made for a long day if the game had not been so exciting.

The game turned out to be one of the most exciting of the season. It looked like Arizona State had the game won when quarterback Jake Plummer scored on a keeper with less than two minutes left, but then substitute sophomore Ohio State quarterback Joe Germaine led a furious Buckeye rally to claim a 20-17 win, spoiling Arizona State's national title hopes. I thought it was interesting that Germaine, who had grown up in nearby Scottsdale, Arizona, and had been a life-long Sun Devils fan, had been offered a scholarship to Arizona State but didn't want to be Plummer's backup. So he went to Ohio State instead and wound up thrusting a dagger in the heart of his boyhood idols.

With the No. 2 team eliminated, it was clear that the next night's Sugar Bowl in New Orleans would decide the national championship.

The next morning, Louise and I had to get up before dawn to catch a 7 a.m. flight to New Orleans to attend the Sugar Bowl. But I'm sure glad we made that flight.

On our way to California several days before, when we changed planes in Dallas, I took the time to call my friend David Johnson, the executive director of the Alabama Music Hall of Fame, to ask his help in locating Percy Sledge. Now that Ann was getting married, Louise kept bugging me about making the call. Those friends I had mouthed off to about knowing good ole Percy were now calling my hand and wanted to know if he was going to sing at Ann and Jamie's May 31st wedding. As far-fetched as it seemed that I could actually line up the singer and back up my big mouth, I got through to David. He said after New Year's, he would call Percy. He would be unable to get in touch with him until then because Percy was performing out of the country.

As we were boarding the plane to New Orleans, Louise turned to me and pointed toward another passenger and said, "Edgar, that looks like Percy Sledge."

Well, I wasn't sure. Could we be that lucky?

As we were taking our seats, I decided to take a chance.

"Percy, my main man!" I yelled out.

He turned around and it was him! Of course, again, he didn't know who I was. I explained my involvement with the Alabama Music Hall of Fame and he told me he was on his way home to Baton Rouge after a New Year's gig in Indonesia.

Well, I started talking about how I had promised to get him to sing at Ann's wedding. Could he do it? So he pulled out a calendar, checked the date and said, yeah, it looked like he could do it then. He handed me a card and told me to call his manager to set it up. After several subsequent telephone calls to his agent, unbelievably, I had signed Percy Sledge to sing at my daughter's wedding. Just like I had said I would. Nothing to it.

After arriving in New Orleans on Thursday afternoon, we spent some time milling around the electric atmosphere of Bourbon Street. Through the years, some of my fondest sporting memories have taken place in New Orleans watching the Sugar Bowl.

When I was a junior at Wetumpka High School, our football team rode a school bus to New Orleans to see the January 1, 1960, Sugar Bowl between LSU and Ole Miss. That was the year when Heisman Trophy winner Billy Cannon made the famous punt return to beat Ole Miss, 7-3, on Halloween, and the Sugar Bowl set up a rematch, where Ole Miss exacted its revenge, 21-0.

The thing that stands out in my mind more than anything else was when my friend Cliff Heard and I went down on the field immediately after the game to try to get Cannon's autograph and he stiff-armed us on the way to meet with some people in the end zone. We later discovered that he was racing to sign a contract with the new American Football League, marking the start of the fierce competition between the two pro leagues.

Most of my memories of the Sugar Bowl involve Alabama. On New Year's Day in 1967, I watched Coach Paul "Bear" Bryant's

Crimson Tide blast Nebraska, 34-7. Quarterback Kenny "Snake" Stabler put on a passing clinic that day. Not only was that arguably Bryant's best football team ever, it was the only time a college program had captured two consecutive national championships, gone undefeated and untied the third year, and been denied the big prize. Alabama went uncrowned and was ranked No. 3, behind national champion Notre Dame and No. 2 Michigan State, who had fought to the infamous 10-10 tie in which Irish coach Ara Parseghian refused to try to win the game at the end. One of the most popular players on that Alabama team was 185-pound tackle Jerry Duncan, who became famous for the tackle eligible play and is now a stockbroker in Birmingham and a good friend of mine.

The memories of that poll robbery remained vivid in the minds of all 'Bama fans seven years later when undefeated, No. 1-ranked Alabama and undefeated, No. 2-ranked Notre Dame met for the first time in the history of the two storied programs in the 1973 Sugar Bowl. It was cold and rainy at old Tulane Stadium that night, and we were all depressed after Notre Dame's 24-23 victory in one of the classic college football games of all time.

As low as I felt that night, I experienced the other end of the spectrum the night Alabama knocked off Miami in the 1993 Sugar Bowl. In those days, the Hurricanes were the biggest bully on the block and practically no one gave Alabama a prayer. But the Crimson Tide shocked everyone and captured its first national title of the post-Bryant era with a 34-14 win. I guess I'll never forget when Alabama defensive back George Teague ran down that Miami receiver and stripped the ball from him. That still ranks as one of the most amazing plays I've ever seen.

Even though this 63rd Sugar Bowl would not involve my favorite team, the atmosphere of the showdown between Florida and Florida State was electric. You could feel it in the air. A month before, the Gators had been ranked No. 1 and lost to No. 2 ranked Florida State, 24-21. The rematch in the Sugar Bowl gave Bobby Bowden and Florida State a chance to wrap up the national championship, but it also gave Steve Spurrier an opportunity at revenge against his arch rival while making a claim for the title. The stakes were huge for both sides.

New Orleans is one of the great places in the world to attend a ball game. The French Quarter, fine dining, major hotels, and entertainment are all within walking distance of the sporting event. The Superdome is a wonderful place to see a game. If the Rose Bowl proved a disappointment in some respects, the Sugar Bowl is always a terrific experience. The seats are comfortable, the concessions are easily accessible and, unlike the Rose Bowl, where you have to park miles away and take a shuttle bus to the stadium, in New Orleans we were able to walk to the Superdome from our hotel.

In an explosive game, Florida quarterback Danny Wuerffel had a tremendous night throwing the football, completing 18 of 34 passes for 306 yards and three touchdowns to lead the Gators' 52-20 victory. Wuerffel had already won the Heisman Trophy and that night he showed why. After a devastating loss to Nebraska in the previous year's Sugar Bowl, Florida finally won its first national championship.

The way the college football bowl system works, Florida was

lucky to get another chance at Florida State, and if it had not gotten the rematch, the Gators could not have vaulted to the title. If Texas had not upset Nebraska in the Big 12 Championship Game, the Cornhuskers would have gone to the Sugar Bowl to play Florida State. Also, if Arizona State had beaten Ohio State in the Rose Bowl, the unbeaten Sun Devils almost certainly would have been awarded the national title over the once-beaten Gators. The final polls showed Florida No. 1, Ohio State No. 2, Florida State No. 3, Arizona State No. 4 and Brigham Young No. 5.

The morning after the Sugar Bowl, Louise flew back to Birmingham and I caught a plane to Green Bay, Wisconsin, to see the 49ers-Packers playoff game. I have always been a Packers fan. One of the reasons was All-Pro quarterback Bart Starr, who was from Montgomery, Alabama, and played for the Crimson Tide before calling the signals for Vince Lombardi's great teams. I've known Bart since he returned to Alabama and he is one of the most respected people in the state. A real class act.

I have also gotten to know Bart, Jr. in recent years. Although Bart, Jr. grew up in Green Bay, he went to the University of Alabama, played on the golf team, and has become a respected Birmingham businessman in his own right. I enjoyed many fine afternoons playing tennis with both junior and senior before injuries started to take their toll on all of us.

After arriving in Green Bay, I drove over to Sammy's Pizza, owned by Steve Crispigna, a college friend of Bart, Jr.'s, who had saved one of Bart's tickets for me. Steve attended high school with Bart in Green Bay, joined him at the University of Alabama and then returned to Green Bay to go into business. He gave me some advice on what kind of clothing to wear to protect myself from the frigid temperatures and directed me to a sporting goods store nearby.

Although the weather was good when I arrived on Friday, a major storm was moving in and the forecast was horrible for Saturday's playoff game. Having spent the last week in California and New Orleans, I arrived in Wisconsin with insufficient clothing for such weather. I went to the sporting goods store and bought long underwear, boots, a wool hat with ear flaps and battery-heated gloves and socks in a futile attempt to stay warm. It was a wonder I didn't electrocute myself. When I got to the checkout counter, the lady told me what I really needed was a rainsuit, so I took her advice and bought an inexpensive clear plastic suit.

The next morning it was cold and rainy; I would be miserable all day. I had to park about half a mile from the stadium and it was freezing. I was trying not to freeze to death but, at the same time, I was really looking forward to seeing a game under such miserable conditions at Lambeau Field in Green Bay, which has this incredible mystique. As I walked toward the stadium, I passed the Don Hutson Practice Facility. Before becoming one of the greatest professional receivers of all time, Hutson had starred at Alabama on the same team with Bear Bryant. That team won the 1934 national championship and beat Stanford in the Rose Bowl.

On my way to the stadium, I had some time to kill and I was looking for a place to get warm, so I decided to tour the Green Bay Packer Hall of Fame. The museum was impressive and one of these days I'd like to go back and spend several hours touring the place. But when I was there, heaters were blasting and I had so much gear on that I suddenly found myself burning up. After spending half an hour in the museum and sweating in my warm clothes, game time was approaching, so I headed out into the cold and walked toward the stadium. Then I started freezing.

Under better weather conditions, the area around Lambeau Field is filled with tailgaters. But on this day, most people were more concerned with warding off frostbite. As I made my way toward the stadium, I finally came upon one small group of hearty tailgaters swigging on Jim Beam bourbon. I could hardly see anything, for my glasses fogging up. I stopped to talk to them and they offered me a swig of whiskey. Since I was beginning to lose feeling in my extremities, I gladly took them up on the offer.

I hadn't noticed, but the blistering wind had ripped right through my rainsuit. Most of the suit had torn off and all I had was one long strip on the outside of my clothes around my mid-section. It looked like a big diaper or a jock strap. I must have been a real sight.

One of the tailgaters looked down at me and said, "Hey, buddy! You're trying to keep that thing warm, aren't you?"

Well, so much for that lady's advice about the cheap rain gear.

When I finally got into the stadium, I had seats right on the 50-yard line. Desmond Howard had two big punt returns that helped the Packers go up 21-7 at the half and 49ers quarterback Steve Young got knocked out early in the game. Behind quarterback Brett Favre, who was on his way to a Super Bowl and MVP season, the Packers claimed a 35-14 victory. The win gave the Packers the home field advantage for the next round of the playoffs, when they would face the winner of the Dallas Cowboys-Carolina Panthers game.

Even though my Green Bay experience was one of the most memorable of the year, I don't think I've ever spent a more miserable day at a sporting event. By the time I got back to my car, I couldn't feel my fingers. A couple of them had turned an eerie shade of white. I actually was fearing frostbite. I was glad to get back to my hotel room and finally get warm.

The next morning, Sunday, January 5, I got up at 4:45 and flew to Charlotte to see the Panthers play the Cowboys. The weather was so bad that I was worried about making it out of Green Bay, but I eventually got out, changed planes in Detroit and arrived in Charlotte. I checked my bags at the airport, caught a cab to the new stadium and watched one of the most exciting games of the year. Unlike Green Bay, the weather was great. After all my travels, I can honestly say that Charlotte's Ericsson Stadium was the nicest open-air football facility that I experienced all year. The amenities were nice and the seats were comfortable and close to the field.

The Cowboys entered the game as the defending Super Bowl Champions and the Panthers were an upstart second-year franchise in the midst of a surprising season. Both teams had Alabama Crimson Tide ties. The Cowboys featured running back Sherman Williams and defensive back George Teague and the Panthers had a backup quarterback named Jay Barker. All three players had helped 'Bama win its last national championship in 1992.

The Dallas team that came to Charlotte that day had been the most dominant franchise of the decade. Before giving way to Barry Switzer, Jimmy Johnson had inherited a team in shambles in the late '80s and rebuilt the Cowboys around three of the biggest stars in the game: quarterback Troy Aikman, running back Emmitt Smith, and wide receiver Michael Irvin. But the Panthers became giant killers that day as the defense intercepted Aikman four times and the offense clicked behind second-year quarterback Kerry Collins, who was starting his first playoff game.

As it turns out, the Panthers knocking off the Cowboys 26-17 that day would mark the end of the Dallas dynasty launched by Jimmy Johnson. The Cowboys have been on the skids ever since. The victory advanced the Panthers to the NFC Championship Game the following week against Green Bay, with the winner going to the Super Bowl.

One guy sitting next to me was a big Dallas fan who got into a fight with some of the Panthers supporters. I had to help break it up, but I didn't mind. I was just glad to be back in the South, where I could actually feel my fingers and my toes. ■

CHAPTER TWO

You Want Me to Put It Where?!

*E*ven though my year was, at the core, a sports fantasy, I wanted to do more than attend sporting events. All my life, I've enjoyed visiting new places and meeting people, so the trip was an extension of my natural curiosity and my determination to see more of the world. Years from now, when I look back on the trip, I'm sure many of the details of the games will fade in my memory. But the people I met and the overall adventure of the experience will stay with me forever.

In the months leading up to my year on the road, it seemed that everyone I met had a suggestion of where I should go and what events I should see. The topic often came up during idle conversation at cocktail parties or civic functions, and I was genuinely interested in the input of anyone who had visited unusual places. Although many of the sporting events I had dreamed about were the ones you might expect — the obvious ones like the Super Bowl, the World Series and the Kentucky Derby — I was determined to load my trip with variety and, if possible, some completely new experiences.

Which is how I came to be in Alaska on the first day of March, freezing half to death but loving every minute of it.

Several months before I embarked on my trip, I was attending a fund-raiser in Washington where I met Laura Payne, a receptionist in the office of Congressman Don Young from Alaska. She started packing my head with talk of her state's greatest sporting event, The Iditarod. Like any other sports fan, of course, I had heard of The Iditarod and harbored some vague notions about it being some sort of race through the frozen wilderness. But beyond that, I was pretty clueless, so the more she talked, the more intrigued I became.

After receiving some detailed information on the race from the congressman's Juneau office, we started digging around and found out that you could actually bid to ride on one of the dogsleds in a pre-race event. Well, that did it. I had to go. This was going to be an experience I could tell my grandchildren about.

The folks who promote The Iditarod call it "the last great race on earth," and after seeing what the competitors must endure, it's difficult to argue with the description. The 1997 race marked the event's 25th anniversary, but the origins of long-distance dogsledding across the Alaskan wilderness run much deeper.

The Iditarod Trail actually began in the 19th century as a mail and supply route from the coastal towns of Seward and Knik to the interior mining camps at Flat, Ohir, and Ruby, and on to the west coast communities of Unalakleet, Elim and Nome. With no other mode of transportation, the dogsleds represented a vital link between the fledgling points of civilization on the Alaskan frontier. Until the airplane arrived on the scene in the early days of this century, the dogsled remained the primary mode of long-distance transportation. The U.S. Postal Service didn't replace its last dogsled team with snowmobiles until 1963.

In 1925, part of the trail became a life-saving highway as an outbreak of diphtheria threatened Nome, with the nearest serum in Anchorage, over a thousand miles away. The serum was packed carefully and placed on the train from Anchorage to the end of the rail line at Nenana, which left 674 more miles to transport the much needed medicine on to Nome. Twenty mushers risked their lives to perform this humanitarian service. The serum arrived safely in Nome on February 2nd. The race today honors this event as well as the history and tradition of mushing.

The Iditarod was born in 1973 as a way to commemorate Alaska's pioneer past. Through the years, the volunteer-run event has grown into one of the most celebrated and unique sporting spectacles in the world, drawing attention from across the globe. Yet it remains exotic because of its location and because most people who live in civilization cannot comprehend the difficulties of racing through the wilderness in the middle of winter.

Each year, beginning around the end of February, about 50 mushers start out with sleds pulled by anywhere from 12 to 16 dogs. The mushers guide the sleds, which sounds simpler than it is, and must be responsible for caring for the dogs as they brave the wilds of the frontier, driving across a 1,150-mile course from Anchorage in south central Alaska to Nome on the western Bering Sea. Most cover the course in nine to 17 days.

Mushers come from all walks of life: fishermen, doctors, business people, and many others. Some train basically year-round for such races; for others, it's strictly a hobby. One of the most fascinating aspects of The Iditarod to me was that it is the only professional sporting event in which men and women compete directly against each other.

One other aspect of the competition sets it apart from all the other events I saw throughout the year. Whereas basketball, basketball and football are primarily games of skill in which the athletes are competing against each other and their own limits, The Iditarod is at the heart a battle against nature. The sub-zero temperatures are a constant strain on the mushers and their dogs and the mushers never know when they will encounter a devastating snow storm, blistering winds or any of nature's other furies while they attempt to negotiate the various steep mountain ranges, dense forests and desolate tundra that form the course. In the days leading up to the race, the mushers must place food and other supplies along the route of the course. Without the proper planning, the mushers and their dogs could starve or freeze to death.

Several years ago, the organizers of the race started something called The Iditarider program, which allows ordinary people to bid for the chance to ride in a sled along a small section of the course. When I heard about that, I was hooked. I never intended my year of sporting events to include any participation, but this was a chance I could not pass up, even though some of my friends thought I was nuts. Maybe. But I was determined to do it anyway. This was going to be my year to make all those dreams come true. No regrets. No second-guessing from my rocking chair 20 years from now.

The Iditarider is operated much like the pro-am portion of a golf tournament. People from throughout the world place bids for the chance to ride with a musher, and all the bid money goes to help defray the cost of the real race.

The folks from Congressman Young's office had referred me to Wrex Diem, who runs The Iditarider program. I bid $800 for the chance to ride, and within a few weeks, I found out that my bid had been selected.

As I started making preparations for the trip, two problems loomed over my ride in a dogsled. In addition to scheduling conflicts, there was the problem with my knee. I had injured my right knee several months before and had undergone arthroscopic surgery, and I was genuinely concerned about being able to sustain the punishment. All the information we had been sent said you had to be "in decent physical shape . . . able to run short distances and have full use of your faculties." Well, if I had had full use of my faculties, I probably wouldn't have been so anxious to run off to Alaska and ride on a dogsled! But that's another story.

After listening to me go on and on about how much I was looking forward to the experience, my good friend John Clements, a Birmingham attorney, sent me a copy of Robert Service's infamous poem "The Cremation of Sam McGee" (see pages 36-40), which spins the harrowing tale of some guy from Tennessee who went to Alaska to pan for gold and wound up dying (perhaps) while mushing across the frozen tundra.

"I am enclosing the classic poem," John wrote, "in hopes this will deter you from your youthful exuberance." (Translation: Edgar, You Fool!)

(Continued on page 41)

THE CREMATION OF SAM McGEE

There are strange things done in the midnight sun
    By the men who moil for gold;
The Arctic trails have their secret tales
    That would make your blood run cold;
The Northern Lights have seen queer sights,
    But the queerest they ever did see
Was that night on the marge of Lake Lebarge
    I cremated Sam McGee.

Now Sam McGee was from Tennessee,
    where the cotton blooms and blows.
Why he left his home in the South to roam
    'round the Pole, God only knows.
He was always cold, but the land of gold
    seemed to hold him like a spell;
Though he'd often say in his homely way
    that "he'd sooner live in Hell."

On a Christmas day we were mushing our way
    over the Dawson trail.
Talk of your cold! through the parka's fold
    it stabbed like a driven nail.
If our eyes we'd close, then the lashes froze
    till sometimes we couldn't see,
It wasn't much fun, but the only one
    to whimper was Sam McGee.

And that very night, as we lay packed tight
    in our robes beneath the snow,
And the dogs were fed, and the stars o'erhead
    were dancing heel and toe,
He turned to me, and "Cap" says he,
    "I'll cash in this trip, I guess;
And if I do I'm asking that you
    won't refuse my last request."

Well, he seemed so low that I couldn't say no;
    then he says with a sort of a moan,
"It's the cursed cold, and it's got right hold
    till I'm chilled clean through to the bone.
Yet 'taint being dead — it's my awful dread
    of the icy grave that pains;
So I want you to swear, that foul or fair,
    you'll cremate my last remains."

A pal's last need is a thing to heed,
    so I swore I would not fail;
And we started on at the streak of dawn;
    but God! he looked ghastly pale.
He crouched on the sleigh, and he raved all day
    about his home in Tennessee;
And before nightfall a corpse was all
    that was left of Sam McGee.

There wasn't a breath in that land of death,
  and I hurried, horror-driven,
With a corpse half hid that I couldn't get rid,
  because of a promise given;
It was lashed to the sleigh, and it seemed to say:
  "You may tax your brawn and brains,
But you promised true, and its up to you
  to cremate these last remains."

Now a promise made is like a debt unpaid,
  and the trail has its own stern code.
In the days to come, though my lips were dumb,
  in my heart how I cursed that load!
In the long, long night, by the lone firelight,
  while the huskies, round in a ring,
Howled out their woes to the homeless snows —
  Oh! God, how I loathed the thing!

And every day that quiet clay
  seemed to heavy and heavier grow;
And on I went, though the dogs were spent
  and the grub was getting low.
The trail was bad, and I felt half mad,
  but I swore I would not give in;
And I'd often sing to the hateful thing,
  and it harkened with a grin.

Till I came to the marge of Lake Lebarge,
 and a derelict there lay;
It was jammed in the ice, but I saw in a trice
 it was called the Alice May.
And I looked at it, and I thought a bit,
 and I looked at my frozen chum;
Then, "Here!" said I, with a sudden cry,
 "is my, cre-ma-tor-eum!"

Some planks I tore from the cabin floor,
 and I lit the boiler fire;
Some coal I found that was lying around,
 and I heaped the fuel higher;
And the flames just soared, and the furnace roared -
 such a blaze you seldom did see,
And I burrowed a hole in the glowing coal,
 and I stuffed in Sam McGee.

Then I made a hike, for I didn't like
 to hear him sizzle so;
And the heavens scowled, and the huskies howled,
 and the wind began to blow.
It was icy cold, but the hot sweat rolled
 down my cheeks, and I don't know why;
And the greasy smoke in an inky cloak
 went streaking down the sky.

I do not know how long in the snow
    I wrestled with grisly fear;
But the stars came out and they danced about
    ere again I ventured near;
I was sick with dread, but I bravely said,
    "I'll just take a peep inside.
I guess he's cooked, and it's time I looked."
    Then the door I opened wide.

And there sat Sam, looking cool and calm,
    in the heart of the furnace roar;
And he wore a smile you could see a mile,
    and he said "Please close that door.
It's fine in here, but I greatly fear
    you'll let in the cold and storm —
Since I left Plumtree, down in Tennessee,
    it's the first time I've been warm."

There are strange things done in the midnight sun
    By the men who moil for gold;
The Arctic trails have their secret tales
    That would make your blood run cold;
The Northern Lights have seen queer sights,
    But the queerest they ever did see
Was that night on the marge of Lake Lebarge
    I cremated Sam McGee.

— Robert W. Service

As our trip to Anchorage neared, we started receiving information from the home office in Alaska about what kind of clothing to wear. They told us temperatures for the program had varied from 45 degrees above zero Fahrenheit to 25 below, and all riders must be prepared for extreme cold. They told us to dress in layers, topped by a parka, heavy boots, mittens instead of gloves (mittens provide more manual dexterity), and a thick hat to cover your ears and help prevent frostbite.

As I read a letter from race manager Jack Niggemyer, I started to get worried about my physical abilities:

"Driving a dog team is not just a matter of standing there and letting the dogs do all the work," Niggemyer said. "It is a very physically taxing job. Running up hills, helping steer the sled around a tight corner and riding the brake on steep slopes are something a musher does routinely every time they hook up a team. As a rider in their sled, you may be asked to do the same. To that end, it is imperative that you be in decent physical shape. Even riding in the sled is not always the most comfortable proposition around. The trails can often be bumpy and rough. You don't have to be a marathon runner, but at the very least you should be able to run short distances and have full use of your faculties . . . "

Considering the condition of my knee, I started worrying about going all that way and not getting to ride. I had this fear in the back of my mind that I wouldn't be able to complete the course. So I started thinking about trying to entice somebody to go with me, someone who could take my place, just in case. Who would be that crazy?

To my surprise, Ann wanted to go with me. Ann is young and healthy and works out all the time. She's in great physical shape, and I knew she would have the stamina that the event demands. More importantly, I thought the trip would provide us with one final father-daughter sports adventure before my little girl got married and started her life with Jamie. As I look back on my life, some of my happiest memories are of coaching my two children in sports. Ann was an outstanding athlete when she was young, and sports has always been a common thread for us as a family.

The problem of conflicting events would confront me time and again throughout the year: I wanted to do it all.

Ever since my days as a University of Alabama student trying to make a little spending money by keeping the official statistics book, I had been enthralled with the annual Alabama State High School Basketball Tournament. As we will discuss later, there's something about watching those kids play in that setting that is incredibly thrilling and unpredictable. But unfortunately, the tournament takes place the last week in February, just like The Iditarod. I would have to miss one or the other, and realizing that the trip to Alaska represented a once-in-a-lifetime opportunity, I reluctantly resigned myself to missing my first state basketball tournament in years.

While sitting in my hotel room in Alaska, oddly enough, I was watching the sports news one day on CNN and what did they show? You guessed it. A clip from the Alabama High School Basketball Tournament. This kid made a shot from three-quarters court in one of the semi-final games to throw it into overtime, and CNN made it their "Play of the Day." I was half a world away and yet, thanks to television . . .

Unfortunately, a week before we were supposed to leave for Alaska, Wrex called my office and left word that my musher, Joe LeFaive, had backed out of the race. I was devastated. Totally crushed. I didn't have a ride. All that time and effort for a once-in-a-lifetime opportunity and I was not going to get to have the experience.

Well, I wasn't going to give up. There had to be some way for me to make this happen. So I called Wrex and shared my frustrations and my determination to ride. After some strategy sessions with several Republican contacts, we decided to approach the GOP mayor of Anchorage, Rick Mystrom, about possibly taking his place in the race. He participated in the program every year, and he was willing to make the sacrifice to help a first-timer from Alabama realize his dream. He gave up his seat to let me race, and I will be forever grateful.

On the way to Alaska, Ann and I flew to Portland and spent half a day touring the city. As we traveled around the city, we discovered what a unique place it is. Portland is a beautiful city bound on the north by the Columbia River. The Willamett River runs through the center of town. Downtown is undergoing a revitalization, like many of the places I visited. The foothills of the Cascade Mountains extend into the city, with Mount St. Helens in the background. There are many parks, walking trails and recreation areas of natural beauty. Portland has several very unique shopping areas with charming specialty stores. Ann and I thought how much Louise would have loved to have been there to go shopping. We visited the campus of Portland State University, a beautiful college in the heart of the city.

After a delightful dinner, we headed to the Rose Garden to see the Trailblazers play the New York Knicks. We got to see one of the premiere centers in the NBA, Patrick Ewing, lead the Knicks to a thrilling, 96-95 victory in overtime. The Knicks rallied from a 15-point deficit in the fourth quarter as Ewing scored 27 points and gathered 14 rebounds. Immediately after the game, some nut called in a bomb threat and they cleared the arena.

The next morning, February 27, Ann and I got up at 4:30 a.m. in order to catch a 6:30 flight to Anchorage on Alaskan Airlines. Someone told me that you could get the best views heading into Alaska on the right side of the plane. Twelve-hundred seventy-nine miles later, we realized they were right. It's a beautiful sight descending into Alaska and seeing the snow-covered mountains, frozen rivers and evergreen trees. The beauty almost defies description.

Even though Alaska became the 49th state in 1959, when I was in high school, it still remains an exotic place for most people in the lower 48. The United States purchased Alaska from the Russian empire in 1867, paying $7.2 million, or about two cents an acre, for a land mass that, if laid on top of the lower 48, would stretch from Jacksonville, Florida, to San Francisco, California. Alaska is more than twice the size of Texas, but it remains sparsely populated. Its population of 603,617 (according to the 1990 census) is only about two-thirds that of metropolitan Birmingham. One in seven Alaskans is an Eskimo, either an American Indian or an Aleut.

We were met at the airport by the Republican National Com-mitteeman from Alaska, Wayne Ross. Wayne and I had met at a GOP function earlier in the year in Washington and he had seemed interested in my trip. He had told me to call him if I was going to make it to The Iditarod, so I did. He dropped us off at our hotel, The Regal Alaskan, which served as the race head-quarters and was located on Lake Hood directly across from the airport.

From the hotel, we had a magnificent view of planes landing both at the airport and on the frozen lake. I was amazed to learn that Lake Hood is the world's busiest float plane base, with over 100,000 takeoffs and landings each year. Only eight percent of the state is accessible by road, which makes air travel a vital transportation link. One in six Alaskans knows how to fly.

The hotel lobby was abuzz with activity. The first thing we saw when we walked into the hotel was a gigantic stuffed polar bear. Ann and I had our picture taken in front of the great white beast and imagined how scary it must be to meet one in the wild.

On our first day in town, we went to a pizza party in the hotel to meet the mushers and our fellow Iditariders. At our table was a fellow Southerner, Dot Magidson of Marietta, Georgia, who also yearned for the experience of a lifetime as an Iditarider. Suddenly, I lost my trepidations about the big ride when I saw a wide variety of ages and physical appearances, both men and women, who were preparing for the adventure. If this attractive, feminine Southern lady could handle the ride, certainly I could.

Her musher, Doug Swingley, a Montana rancher and dog breeder, had claimed first place in 1995 and finished second in the 1996 race. Like many of the top mushers, Swingley trains year-round and participates in sled races in states such as Minnesota, Michigan and Montana. Doug is a professional musher and it was very enlightening hearing that side of the event. The professional mushers are just as fit and conditioned as any other athletes in terms of endurance and strength.

In contrast, my musher, William Edgar Bass, is an amateur who races for the adventure and sport. A former minor league baseball player, Bass, who ironically shares my first and middle names, owns his own food brokerage business and has been mushing since 1992. Bill was born in Portland, Oregon, in 1947. After graduating from Oregon State University in 1969, he and his wife Cheryl moved to Alaska to explore the last great frontier. Bill served as an officer in the Alaska National Guard and, like so many Alaskans, is an experienced pilot.

Unlike many of the mushers, who looked like they were pulled from a Jack London novel, with long beards and hair, Bill looked like a businessman yanked from a day at the office. Which is exactly what he was.

That night, we attended The Iditarod XXV Mushers Banquet and Drawing at the Sullivan Arena, where we got to mingle and watch the mushers draw for positions. Susan Butcher, a four-time winner of the race in the late 1980s and early '90s who would not be competing this year, served as emcee, underscoring how this event represents such a unique stage for men and women to race on equal footing.

The man often called "the father of The Iditarod," Joe Reddington, Sr., was awarded honorary first position. Now 80 years old, Joe had been instrumental in launching the race in 1973. In fact, he worked so hard in that inaugural year, he did not get the opportunity to race. This would be his 19th Iditarod as a contestant; he had finished fifth four times. I really enjoyed meeting Joe and grew to admire his determination to race at his age.

The next day, Ann and I took time to do some sight-seeing around the area. We traveled to the Alyeska Resort at the base of Mt. Alyeska, a beautiful place frequented by skiing enthusiasts of all skill levels. We saw Portage Glacier and Explorer Glacier in the Chugach National Forest.

Our tour guide, Joe Lester, shared many interesting facts about the history of Alaska and modern life in our 49th state. I was fascinated to learn about Alaska's Permanent Fund, generated by the 800-mile-long Trans-Alaska Pipeline from the Arctic Coastal Plain at Prudhoe Bay to Valdez, where the oil is placed on tankers. Thanks to the foresight of several politicians more than 30 years ago, the state of Alaska has been able to amass a fund of more than $22 billion from the sale of oil rights. Given Alaska's history of allowing outsiders to profit from various natural resources with little or no return to the state, in 1976 voters approved a constitutional amendment establishing the fund. Half of the money is reinvested and half is paid out to the state's citizens each year, like dividends in a corporation. Each year, each citizen of Alaska (regardless of age) receives a check as annual compensation for those rights, which varies based upon investment results. It has never been less than $1,000.00, and in 1997, it exceeded $1,400.00 per person. If only more governments could work that way.

That afternoon, we went back to Anchorage and got a chance to have an up-close visit with one of the dog teams. I thought the dogs might be vicious, but they were very friendly and let us pet them. We got to sit on the sled and even take a short practice run if we wanted. The experience gave us all a comfort level with what we were about to do.

That night, we attended the fourth annual "Fun Raiser," an auction of Iditarod memorabilia. The proceeds help defray the cost of running the event.

Every year, the mushers take several envelopes which they get stamped by the postal service at the start of the race in Anchorage and then at the finish in Nome. These envelopes are popular items at the auction, so I bought three, including one of Joe Reddington's, the father of The Iditarod, one of Jeff King's, a multi-time winner of the event, and one of DeeDee Jonrowe's, who holds the women's speed record with the fourth-fastest Iditarod time ever. I also bought one of Joe's musher bibs. He was kind enough to sign it for me.

One of the most interesting people I met was a local named Ted Millette. I met him through a friend of Ted's wife, Lila Peters of Utah, who was an Iditarider like me.

In 1989, Ted was featured on Oprah Winfrey's program, "Single Men in Alaska." The purpose of the show was to encourage women to move to Alaska. Most of the men were in their 20s and 30s, except for Ted, who was in his 60s and had been divorced for 17 years.

While on a layover in Toronto, several Eastern Airlines flight attendants were watching the show, and called their single friend Linda into the room to watch. Linda, a native of Georgia, was impressed with Ted and finally mustered up enough courage to call him.

After the show aired, Ted was swamped with more than 200 letters and telephone calls from single women all over the United States. He eventually talked with several women and even had a few dates, but there were no sparks. Until Linda.

The first time Linda called, much to her dismay, Ted was out of town. Ted's next-door neighbor happened to answer Linda's call when she was watering the plants and feeding the cat. Ironically, Ted's neighbor also happened to be his ex-wife. She encouraged Ted to call Linda back. Finally, Ted called Linda and, after a long telephone conversation, they decided to try to get to know each other better. Linda sent her picture to Ted and one thing led to another. Eastern Airlines went on strike and Linda took advantage of her time off by flying to Alaska to visit Ted. Several months later, the couple married in Kauai, Hawaii.

I knew it would be incredibly cold in Alaska, so I went out and bought what I thought would be adequate clothing for the event before we left Birmingham. But I discovered I wasn't quite prepared, so on the day before our race, I went out and bought some even warmer clothes. And I was still freezing.

After several months of planning and anticipation, I woke up early on the morning of March 1, the day of The Iditaride. I was a little nervous and anxious for my big day. My adrenaline was pumping. Ann and I caught a cab to downtown Anchorage and they had the whole area cleared out and secured. You had to have credentials to get inside this eight-block area. What an incredible sight. There were 52 mushers there with their dogs, 12 to 16 dogs per musher, and the dogs were all barking like crazy because they train their whole lives to race, and when the mushers hook them up, they know it's time to perform. You can imagine the noise.

The dogs are treated like thoroughbred race horses. The majority of the sled dogs are Huskies. The mushers know they are totally dependent on their dogs to pull them through the wilderness, so they treat them with the greatest care, including laying down straw when they rest to insulate them from the cold ground. Contrary to my expectations of fat, bushy-looking animals, the dogs were lean and neat, with the well-toned bodies of athletes. Some had long hair, some short. They were all colors. Some wore tiny booties to protect their feet from the cold, hard snow.

It was an incredibly beautiful day, about 15 degrees and sunny. We were lucky to have such good weather. After we all walked around and visited for a while, we were told to line up and take our places. Then I saw Bill Bass's truck with all of his sponsors' names on the sides. That's when I got a little nervous. The lettering at the top of the truck read: Crazy Bill "Scooter" Bass. All of a sudden, I wanted to know: Why did they call him crazy?

As we got strapped in, Bill pulled out this huge, sharp, three-pronged hook that is used to stop the sled. He said, "You're gonna have to hold this between your legs. If I need it to stop the sled you'll have to hand it to me." Now I knew why they called him crazy!

In all that time looking at the other sleds, I never saw another hook. I looked at him like he was nuts. I was scared to death. This was a really sharp hook, suddenly located in a very sensitive position. My mind started racing. I had heard all the stories about sleds going airborne and turning over. I figured if that happened to us, that hook would either kill me or castrate me. I had flashes of having to go back to Birmingham and explain why I had left part of my original equipment on the frozen tundra.

I was suddenly very nervous about the whole thing, but I couldn't back out now. The teams left every two minutes, and pretty soon, they were calling our team. Before I could think much more about the possibilities, they called my name and they brought us up to the starting line, which was draped with a larger banner hanging above the street. Several thousand spectators lined the path.

"Edgar Welden!" the announcer shouted as the crowd roared. "Edgar Welden from Birmingham, Alabama! . . . "

For a moment, I felt like they were calling my name during pre-game introductions at the Super Bowl.

Then we were off, mushing through downtown Anchorage and then out into the suburbs, through a beautiful park and eventually out into the countryside.

We would cover 15 miles over about 75 minutes, roughly the pace of a good marathon runner. As we passed one area, some locals passed us muffins, like marathoners being handed cups of water.

Eventually, we started mushing through an area that was a little rough and we went through this narrow passage with a pretty steep slope. We actually turned over. Well, I was keeping my hand and my eyes on that hook the whole time. Just as the sled turned over, I threw that hook out of the way and tumbled out of the sled, rolling about three or four feet. Thank goodness, the hook went one way and I went the other. Bill and I gathered ourselves, I got back on the sled and we went on our way.

Our race ended way out in the countryside. They had a warm trailer set up for us, complete with fresh coffee, and I started to thaw out a little. A bus took us back into Anchorage. I can still feel that incredible cold. After being out in the raw for 75 minutes, I could hardly feel my toes. I did not want to imagine what it would be like to be out there for 10 days, like the competitors.

Even with the hook, I must say the experience was one of the most memorable of my life. The truth is, the fear associated with having a sharp metal prong dangling between my legs probably enhanced the experience. I may not know what it's like to be 500 miles out in the middle of nowhere and go tumbling down a mountainside wondering if anyone will ever see me again, but a little bit of fear can go a long way.

That night, the state Republican Party was holding its annual Lincoln Day fund-raising banquet, so naturally, they were happy for me to attend. Senator Frank Murkowski was the speaker. I met all these local Republicans who couldn't believe I had come all the way from Alabama to race in the Iditaride. Finally, I met Mayor Rick Mystrom. I thanked him for allowing me to take his ride, and giving me such a wonderful memory.

The next morning, after Ann had returned to Birmingham, I went down to breakfast and started planning how I was going to see the start of the real race, The Iditarod. Because the weather around Anchorage was unusually mild (not to me!), they had moved the start of the race about 50 miles north to the village of Willow. I was preparing to take a bus to see the start, but at breakfast, I met a reporter from The Detroit Free Press, Patricia Chargot, who was fascinated by my trip. She had a rental car and kindly offered to let me ride with her.

It was a beautiful drive through the countryside, and though watching the race had a kind of anticlimactic feel after my own personal adventure the day before, it was a real experience to see the start. Even though they had moved the start of the race, the first mile of the route was lined with thousands of spectators. Every time a musher zoomed by, the whole crowd would cheer. It was an electric atmosphere.

One of the mushers I had met was a fellow Southerner named Sonny King, a veterinarian from Spartanburg, South Carolina. Several years before, someone had given Sonny an Alaskan Malamute, which got him interested in arctic breeds and, eventually, in mushing. One thing led to another and Sonny started volunteering as a vet for The Iditarod, which gradually filled him with the desire to train and race his own dog-sled team. He bought a whole team of sled dogs, which he keeps in Montana, and started training for races, even as he continued to work as a vet for The Iditarod, winning the "Golden Stethoscope" award in 1996 from The Iditarod Official Finishers Club for his exemplary care of the dogs. Finally, in 1997, after years of hard work and anticipation, he would have the chance to mush.

Prior to the start of the race, I was inside having coffee and talking with the people around me. A nice lady standing nearby noticed my Southern accent.

"Excuse me," she said. "Where are you from . . . ?"

I told her I was from Alabama. She turned out to be Mrs. Sara King, Sonny King's mother, who had traveled with her daughter from Georgia to see her son's big day. She was very anxious and apprehensive about Sonny's first ride in The Iditarod.

After watching all of the teams head out into the wilderness, Pat and I started back toward Anchorage and stopped on the way to tour an old Russian Orthodox church and cemetery. The church is similar to the ones scattered throughout the Russian countryside and reminded me of Alaska's non-American roots. Beside it was an ancient cemetery where the Athabascon Indians constructed "spirit houses" on the graves of their ancestors. The miniature houses are ornate and colorful.

In the days when the mushers and their dogs were carrying goods and the mail, long before snowmobiles and airplanes, the mushers had a unique way of relaying word that they were on the trail. It was similar to the way pilots will file a flight plan, just in case they come up missing. In those days, a kerosene lamp was hung outside roadhouses along the trail. The lamps were not extinguished until the musher and his team reached their destination. The day when the race starts in Anchorage, a lamp called a widow's lamp is lit at the trail's end in Nome. It is not put out until the last musher reaches Nome.

Over the next several days, as I was back in the lower 48

attending other sporting events, I monitored the progress of the mushers with a sense of longing. My musher, "Crazy Bill," finished 38th and was awarded the AC Sterling Achievement Award, voted by his peers the most improved musher. Martin Buser won the race with a time of 9 days, 8 hours, 30 minutes and 45 seconds and won a $50,000 prize. Joe Reddington, Sr., the 80-year-old father of The Iditarod, finished 36th.

One of the most inspiring stories I saw all year involved musher DeeDee Jonrowe. Her determination to compete in The Iditarod despite incredible odds was one of the greatest feats of athletic achievement I witnessed on my tour.

Months before the race, DeeDee was driving through the countryside in her car with her husband Mike and her grandmother, when the vehicle was hit head-on by a truck on a bridge. Her grandmother was killed and Mike was left critically injured, with severe head trauma. DeeDee also sustained serious injuries. No one expected her to return to competition.

But DeeDee, who already held the women's speed record for The Iditarod, was determined to race in 1997. Miraculously, she worked her way back into top physical shape and finished fourth in The Iditarod. To this day, I am still amazed that anyone could be in a serious car accident mere months before enduring the elements for nine days in the wilderness, mushing through some of the most unforgiving terrain in the world, much less placing fourth in the competition.

DeeDee credits the Alaskan "family" of volunteers, mushers and natives for aiding her recovery. She talks with pride about the incredible sense of oneness among all the people involved with The Iditarod. Like so many of the competitors, she praises the dogs and stresses the need to provide a good quality of life for the animals, whom she compares to marathon runners. I enjoyed meeting this classy, sharp, attractive woman who also happened to be an outstanding athlete and stood out from the majority of the mushers, who tended to be burly men.

Someday, I would like to return to Alaska and see the mushers finish the race in Nome. But this time, after watching the start, I headed back to the South. It was basketball season, and there were tournaments to watch. ■

CHAPTER THREE

Full Court Press

No other sporting event excites me like a basketball tournament. Nowhere else in sports is the pressure and emotion so intensely focused on the outcome of one game. Win and you get to keep playing, perhaps for a trophy somewhere down the line. Lose and you go home. Regardless of whether the players are high school students or millionaire professionals, you can see the competitors raise the level of their game as they try desperately to stay alive. A basketball tournament is as much about adrenaline and determination as it is about scoring and rebounding.

Nowadays, when tournament time rolls around, high school athletes often have the added incentive of playing for college scholarships and college athletes want to impress the pro scouts. I remember feeling the pressure of playing in tournaments and wanting to keep playing, but my experience was a little different. If we were playing a tournament on Friday night and won, I did not have to work at my daddy's grocery store on Saturday. He would let me off to rest up. But if we lost, I had to go to work as usual. Instead of having the chance to score a game-winning basket, I would be in a bad mood and have to listen to my daddy yell at me to quit putting the bread and the eggs in the bottom of the grocery sack.

Incentive to win comes in all shapes and sizes!

On my year-long adventure, I experienced basketball at all levels, both regular season and tournament games, both men and women, high school, college and professional. I saw a total of 90 basketball games, which represents about one-third of all the sporting events on my schedule. (Over two-thirds of those games were tournament or playoff games.) By comparison, the average college team plays about 30 games and the pros play a grueling 82-game regular season schedule. When you add all those games together, I saw more action than the men's teams at Alabama and Auburn combined.

My first exposure to college basketball came at Garrett Coliseum in the 1950s when I would go to see Alabama and Auburn play each other or against Adolph Rupp's dominant Kentucky program. In those days, my favorite team was Joel Eaves' Auburn Tigers, during the days of the so-called "seven dwarfs."

Over the last two decades, I've been a season ticket holder to Alabama basketball, watching the Tide in times both good and bad. What 'Bama fan could forget the night during the 1976 NCAA Mideast Regional at Baton Rouge when C.M. Newton's Tide gave undefeated Indiana a scare before losing to Bobby Knight's eventual national champions? Or Wimp Sanderson's great teams in the '80s and early '90s?

During the regular season, I concentrated on college basketball and saw games involving many of the top programs. I saw Indiana crush Penn State in Bloomington, Indiana, where many were starting to wonder about Bobby Knight's future. I witnessed tensions flare at West Lafayette, Indiana, where eventual Big Ten champ Minnesota edged Purdue after a fight broke out among the players. I was there for the South Carolina upset of Kentucky in overtime at Columbia, a key milepost on the Gamecocks' SEC championship season, and saw Cincinnati claim a victory at home over Tulane, where I was surprised that they sold beer. I was there when UAB defeated Memphis in the dedication game of Bartow Arena. I watched the Big East race start to take shape as Boston College knocked off towel-clutching John Thompson's Georgetown Hoyas at Boston, and was there to see Duke snap a nine-game losing streak to Wake Forest in Winston-Salem, where my niece Jennifer Welden accompanied me to the game.

At the start of the 1997-98 season, I also traveled to Chicago to see the Great Eight tournament, where Kansas knocked off defending national champions Arizona, Kentucky defeated Purdue and North Carolina beat Louisville.

While tournament basketball holds a special place in my heart, I enjoyed crisscrossing the country during the regular season and getting to see games at some of the legendary venues. A month into my trip, I traveled to Durham, North Carolina, with my friend John McMahon to see Coach Mike Kryzewski's Blue Devils host Coach Dean Smith's North Carolina Tar Heels. After watching all those games, I can honestly say that no arena in college basketball can compare to ancient Cameron Indoor Stadium on the Duke campus, which reeks of history in contrast to the antiseptic new facilities like the Dean Dome. Even though the bench seats, which have no backs, are narrow and uncomfortable, the place emotes an unmistakable feeling of tradition. It was the loudest place I have ever been in my life. Several times during the game, John and I tried to communicate with each other, but the noise was so intense, we couldn't hear each other shout even though we were sitting side-by-side.

When Duke takes the court, Cameron, which seats only 9,314 fans, becomes a place of ultimate intimidation for the opposing team. I was told that students sometimes camp outside the arena for two days in "Kryzewskiville" to land precious seats for the next game. The fans, especially the students known as the Cameron Crazies, unmercifully taunt the opposing players over everything from poor shooting to low SAT scores. They chant in unison like a well-rehearsed chorus, swaying back-and-forth with the precision of a drill team, standing up the whole game. Legend holds that Cameron was the birthplace of the "airball!" chant.

After being the most successful program in college basketball in the early '90s, winning consecutive national championships in 1991 and '92, Duke had fallen on hard times, losing seven straight to its archrival. Coach K had suffered through some health problems and had considered retiring. So when Duke came from behind to stage an 80-73 victory, which marked the beginning of a turnabout for the program, the fans stormed the court and cut down the nets. I was surprised by the scene. All those great years and those Duke fans were so worked up by beating North Carolina! It was clear to me that the North Carolina-

Duke basketball rivalry is every bit as intense as the Alabama-Auburn football rivalry.

Seeing North Carolina several times throughout the year allowed me to watch the progression of the Tar Heels from mediocre to national championship contender. In mid-January, when I traveled to the Dean Dome in Chapel Hill to see North Carolina play North Carolina State, the Tar Heels were an uncharacteristic 0-3 in Atlantic Coast Conference play. Even though Smith was within striking distance of Adolph Rupp's all-time victory record, the fans were on his back. But the N.C. State game would prove to be a turning point as the Tar Heels stormed from behind to score the final 12 points and claim a hard-fought 59-56 victory. It was interesting to see a young team start to mature toward the middle of the season. Highly-recruited sophomores Antawn Jamison and Vince Carter finally began playing up to their potential, and freshman point guard Ed Cota cut down on his turnovers, developing into a solid floor leader.

Entering the season, Dean Smith needed 26 victories to break Rupp's record. When the Tar Heels opened their ACC season with three consecutive losses, it looked as though the record chase might be pushed back to the following season. But the story of North Carolina's turnaround, which I witnessed, also turned out to be the last great chapter of a legendary coaching career.

Ever since the Southeastern Conference renewed its post-season tournament in 1979, my family has attended almost every year. As much as I have enjoyed the SEC tournament, the ACC tournament has long been considered the premier conference tournament in the country, so I had to go. After watching the first day of the SEC tournament in Memphis, I caught a flight to Greensboro, North Carolina, to attend my first ACC tournament. My hosts for the weekend were friends from Tampa, Bert and Teddy Salem. They are avid North Carolina fans and made certain I experienced every aspect of this great tournament. We also got to visit during the tournament with Dr. Tom Hearn, the president of Wake Forest University, who had been on the faculty at UAB.

The most important difference between the ACC tournament and all the rest is the quality of competition. The top two or three teams in the ACC usually are contending to be No. 1 seeds in one of the NCAA regionals, and one or more often wind up advancing to the Final Four. Even more significant is the quality of the conference from top to bottom. It's not uncommon for seven or eight of the nine teams in the ACC to qualify for post-season play.

Unlike the SEC, where perhaps three-quarters of all the fans in attendance are rooting for either Kentucky or Arkansas, the ACC is like an annual homecoming for the alumni of all nine teams. You can see this festival atmosphere between sessions of the tournament, when thousands of fans from all of the schools congregate in an adjoining civic center to drink, eat and breathe basketball. Each school organizes a party for their fans.

One of the greatest aspects of tournament basketball is the unpredictable nature of the beast. On a good night, any team can get lucky. It was thrilling for me to watch eighth-seeded North Carolina State upset top-seeded Duke in the opening round (the first time that's ever happened) and advance to the finals against second-seeded North Carolina. When North Carolina defeated North Carolina State in the finals, 64-54, it clinched more than another ACC tournament championship for the Tar Heels. The victory also moved Dean Smith closer to the record.

After winning the ACC tournament, North Carolina was awarded the No. 1 seed in the NCAA East Regional and would play its first two games at Joel Coliseum in Winston-Salem, North Carolina, which was the equivalent of a home-court advantage. Smith needed two victories to surpass Adolph Rupp's record, which had once seemed as unattainable as Babe Ruth's 714 home runs and Amos Alonzo Stagg's 314 football coaching victories.

In the long and storied history of college basketball, no name is more revered than Adolph Rupp. In 41 seasons at the University of Kentucky, the so-called Baron won 876 games and lost 190. His teams dominated the Southeastern Conference like no man before or since. In college basketball, he remains an almost mythical figure whose legend has only been enhanced by the passage of time. Each year, The Birmingham Tip-Off Club awards the Rupp Cup Award to the SEC Coach of the Year.

After defeating Fairfield in the first round, which allowed Smith to tie the record, North Carolina faced ninth-seeded Colorado, which had upset Bobby Knight and Indiana. Much like the 1981 Alabama-Auburn football game, when Paul "Bear" Bryant stood on the verge of surpassing Stagg, the North Carolina-Colorado game became a national media event in which the tournament took a backseat to history. It also reinforced the aspects I enjoy so much of college basketball and tournament play. Everything was riding on one game. If North Carolina had lost, the record chase would have been pushed back to the following season, when the Tar Heels were scheduled to open in the Alaska Shoot-out in Anchorage, four thousand miles from Chapel Hill. What a tragedy that would have been!

After watching the first round Southeastern Regional games in Charlotte, I drove to Winston-Salem to witness the record-breaking game. I went to the arena and spent an hour scouting around for a ticket, because I knew the record chase would make the game a hard sellout. Finally, I got lucky and found a ticket. I had some time to kill, so I called my niece Jennifer. Jennifer, who attended Wake Forest, is a physician's assistant to a heart surgeon and is a huge basketball fan; in fact, she officiates girl's basketball in the Winston-Salem area. She and several of her friends met me for a pre-game meal and then Jennifer and I went to the game, where we watched one of the most suspenseful games of the year. After leading by only one point at the half, North Carolina went on a 30-8 run midway through the second half and buried Colorado, 73-56, to give Dean Smith the record.

Even though the national media hyped the game beyond belief, and dozens of Smith's former players flew in from around the country to witness the historic moment, I found it very interesting that Dean Smith downplayed the whole affair. He's a real class act. Sometimes, nice guys do finish first.

At various times throughout my trip, my friends marveled at my good fortune. The ticket I had bought on the street for the record-breaking game turned out to be an NBA scout's seat on the floor, right behind one of the baskets and adjacent to the North Carolina bench, which gave me a great view of Dean Smith the entire game. Near the start of the game, I looked up into the stands at mid-court and made eye contact with my friends Bert and Teddy Salem and Elaine Sandman, three of the biggest North Carolina fans in the world. They couldn't believe my luck.

 What Do Governor George Pataki, Coach Lute Olson and Edgar Welden Have in Common?

We were all at the Mountain Brook Inn on Sunday, March 23rd, 1997, when politics, basketball, and my agitated family collided.

I had just returned that morning from my trip to the historic final open classification Indiana high school basketball tournament. The whole family was planning to meet me for a quiet lunch, a rarity during a year when I spent most of my time rushing from place to place attending sporting events.

On my way to lunch I stopped by the Mountain Brook Inn, which our company owns, to check on business and make sure everything was running smoothly. That turned out to be a big mistake.

In addition to hosting the University of Arizona basketball team, which was playing in the Southeast Regional that weekend at the Birmingham-Jefferson Civic Center, the hotel was also the site of a fund-raiser sponsored by a group of local Republicans on behalf of New York Governor George Pataki, who was in the midst of a five-city Southern tour. Some weeks earlier, the local sponsors of the event had asked me to serve as one of the hosts of the fund-raiser, given my role as Republican National

Committeeman. However, given my hectic sports schedule, I had declined.

As I was getting ready to leave the hotel and meet my family for lunch, one of the sponsors insisted on me staying for the function. Some of the party faithful who had purchased tickets for the luncheon could not attend at the last minute and they needed us to fill their places. I reluctantly called my family and they reluctantly agreed to come over to the hotel, knowing that our rare family quality time had just evaporated. They were not happy.

While I was waiting for my family to arrive, the manager of the hotel, Jeff Rothstein, rushed up to me and said frantically, "Edgar, we have a problem!"

Jeff informed me that there was a group of demonstrators in front of the hotel. It turned out that they were protesting Governor Pataki's recent decision to remove the Georgia flag from the area surrounding the New York state capitol in Albany. Worse, Jeff said, one of the local TV stations had shown up to cover the demonstration for the evening news.

About that same time, the Arizona basketball team and head coach Lute Olson and his wife were walking through the lobby heading to their pre-game meal. I could not help being concerned that the Wildcats, who were getting ready to play the biggest game of their lives, with a trip to the Final Four riding in the balance, would be distracted by the disturbance.

A short time later, my family walked into the lobby. Their displeasure with me showed. Once again, I had coerced them into attending yet another political function when all they wanted to do was have a quiet family lunch.

While I was catching hell from my family, one of the local sponsors of the fund-raiser rushed up to me breathlessly and demanded, "Edgar! I want you to have those demonstrators arrested and removed before Pataki arrives!"

I told him I thought that would be a mistake.

A short time later, I was getting ready to head for the Pataki meeting room, where the other attendees were waiting for the guest of honor. As luck would have it, Pataki walked in and there I was. And so were the TV cameras. On the evening news that night, the cameras showed the protesters, Pataki, and me. I wasn't even supposed to be there!

I mentioned to Governor Pataki that the Arizona basketball team was staying at the hotel that weekend and that they were having their pre-game meal. On his way to his own function, he stopped by to wish them well in their game against Providence that afternoon.

When the governor and I walked into the meeting room, I could not help being a little paranoid. I noticed some of the sponsors of the event motioning toward the table where my family was seated. The Welden party had already started eating, but naturally, since I had not planned on being on hand for the event, I had declined to register for lunch. The sponsors, who I imagined were questioning the presence of my family, didn't know I was doing a favor for my friend by trying to help them fill the room. So in order to avoid looking like a cheapskate, I wrote a check for a contribution.

After the function, as we were leaving to go to the ballgame, the hotel manager came up to me and said the Arizona athletic director had just called from the Civic Center, where the team was getting ready for its game, to say Coach Olson had misplaced his Final Four ring from an earlier season. A subsequent inspection of his room by the housekeeping staff turned up the missing ring, and Jeff personally delivered it to the athletic director at the Civic Center before game time.

That afternoon, Arizona knocked off Providence in overtime to advance to the Final Four.

I was delighted when everyone left town happy.

I've always loved the movie "Hoosiers," which depicted a basketball team from a tiny Indiana high school beating the odds and winning the state championship while facing teams from much larger schools. The classic 1986 motion picture, which starred Gene Hackman, was a fictionalized account of the real-life drama in which Milan High School, with an enrollment of 162 students, captured the state title in 1954. Bobby Plump canned a 15-foot shot at the buzzer, forever cementing his status as a Hoosier hero. It was the ultimate tale of David slaying Goliath, inspiring countless American boys and girls with the notion that anything is possible. Dreams, indeed, could come true.

When I started planning my trip, attending the 87th annual Indiana High School Athletic Association Boys Basketball State Finals was high on my list. After all, nowhere in the country is the game played with such devotion and reverence. In the months leading up to the 87th annual tournament, however, the Indiana High School Athletic Association voted, after rigorous and heated debate, to discard the open classification tournament — the last of its kind in the nation — in favor of creating four separate tournaments based on enrollment. I had the chance to see the end of an era in American sports.

The four teams who advanced to the RCA Dome in Indianapolis faced the incredible challenge of playing two games in one day, which placed a premium on endurance. After the semifinals at 10:30 a.m. and 12:30 p.m., the championship game at 8 p.m. was played in front of a crowd of some 26,000, in addition to a state-wide television audience. As I watched the championship game, one of the weaknesses of the old format was easy to see. Delta had advanced to the final after an emotionally draining semifinal victory over LaPorte, and appeared so tired, the team failed to score a single point in the first quarter of the final. Bloomington North easily handled Delta, 75-54, to win the last open classification tournament in Indiana high school history.

The electric atmosphere reminded me of the NCAA Final Four, which was appropriate. The next week, the Final Four would be played on the very same court. In 1998, the first year of the new classification format, attendance for the Indiana High School Tournament would plummet by 21.6 percent.

The high schools in Alabama have six classifications, which means six different communities get to celebrate the accomplishment of winning the state championship. It's wonderful to see that many young people be able to go home champions. The Indiana experience represented the other extreme and, in a larger sense, the stuff of dreams. If I'd had a vote, I would have voted to keep the one open classification. Each state is different and what is best for Indiana may not be right for another state.

Five days later, after the Pataki controversy and squeezing in a trip to the Lipton Tennis Tournament in Miami, the Miami-Vancouver NBA game and the NCAA Southeast Regional in Birmingham, I returned to Indianapolis with my mother, wife, and sister for the Final Four. It was my mother's first trip to the NCAA Final Four, even though she has always been a huge basketball fan. With the hotels in Indianapolis demanding a four-night minimum, we decided to stay in Cincinnati instead, which worked out fine and allowed us to also catch the Women's Final Four in Cincinnati and commute the two hours to Indianapolis.

Five years before, John Clements, the president of The Birmingham Tip-Off Club, had appointed me to chair a committee to study the feasibility of bringing a post-season high school tournament to Birmingham. Working with Dan Washburn, the executive director of the Alabama High School Athletic Association, and his capable staff, we were able to convince the AHSAA Central Board of Control to change the format of their state championship tournaments. In previous years, the boys' and girls' tournaments for all six classifications had been scattered around the state. Under the new format, we developed a plan to bring the final four teams for boys and girls in each classification to Birmingham. The event, contested at the 17,000-seat Birmingham-Jefferson Civic Center, is the only one of its kind in the nation where both girls and boys teams compete at the same venue during the same week. I can't say enough about the volunteers from The Birmingham Tip-Off Club who help make the tournament possible, as well as our full-time executive director, Lynne Keller, and the AHSAA's Dan Washburn, Jimmy Cal, and their outstanding staff.

The high school final four, which is run by the non-profit Alabama Basketball Foundation, has blossomed into a tremendous success, even attracting state-wide television coverage of both boys' and girls' championship games, particularly raising the level of awareness of girls basketball in Alabama to unexpected heights. Building on the solid foundation laid by long-time AHSAA executive director Herman L. "Bubba" Scott, Dan Washburn has done an excellent job in taking high school athletics in Alabama to a new level.

When I was in high school, girls only played basketball in gym class. In recent years, however, due to my involvement with the Alabama high school tournament, I have become a big fan of girls' and women's basketball.

In June, I traveled to Los Angeles to see the first game of the Women's National Basketball Association between the Los Angeles Sparks and the New York Liberty. In terms of history, New York's 67-57 victory may turn out to have been one of the most significant events I attended all year. The existence of a women's professional league suddenly means girls all across America can aspire, like boys, to make a living playing basketball. It was touching to see the large number of mothers and daughters sitting among the 14,284 fans at the Forum that afternoon, realizing that a new era had dawned in the history of women's athletics.

It has been amazing to watch the transformation of women's basketball over the last decade. Once I thought it was slow and dull, but now it is an increasingly fast-paced and exciting game.

While we watched the Women's Final Four in Cincinnati on Friday night, March 28, it was impossible not to notice the high quality of the women's game. We saw the Old Dominion women upset Stanford in overtime, 83-82, followed by defending national champion Tennessee's 80-66 victory over Notre Dame. Then, on Saturday, we drove to Indianapolis to watch the national men's semi-finals, where Arizona defeated North Carolina, 66-58, which turned out to be the final game of Dean Smith's legendary career, and Kentucky knocked off Minnesota, 78-69. Then we drove back to Cincinnati, arriving after midnight. I was tired, but my 79-year-old mother was ready for more.

On Sunday, after watching Tennessee capture its second straight national championship — and fifth overall under head coach Pat Summitt — with a 68-59 victory over Old Dominion before 16,700 fans, we returned to Indianapolis the next day to see the final college game of the year. Arizona claimed an 84-79 victory over Kentucky in the men's final, which proved to be Rick Pitino's last game as the UK head coach.

The television announcers credited Arizona's strong defense and impressive outside shooting for the victory. But all of us at the Mountain Brook Inn know better. We're convinced that it was all that wonderful Southern hospitality afforded the Wildcats during their stay at our hotel in Birmingham.

On the day of the men's national championship game, as we drove from Cincinnati to Indianapolis, we took a detour off the interstate and visited Milan High School, where we could feel the history in the air, especially considering the last open classification high school tournament which I had seen the previous week. Somebody told us about Bobby Plump's restaurant in Indianapolis, so on the way to the RCA Dome we went by Plump's Last Shot for a pre-game meal of hamburgers and chicken fingers. I enjoyed looking at all the photographs and souvenirs from Milan's legendary year.

A year later, while I was visiting Indianapolis on a site selection trip for the Republican National Committee, Plump was part of the welcoming delegation. The city was one of the finalists to host the 2000 Republican National Convention, and like all the rest, the officials were pulling out all the stops to impress us and attract the biggest event in the history of Indianapolis. It was interesting to me that after more than 40 years, the hero of that shot heard around the world remains a giant in Indiana. Bobby and I had lunch together, where I challenged him to a game of HORSE at the Hinkle Fieldhouse on the campus of Butler University, the site of his famous shot and where they filmed the movie. I am looking forward to our game one day.

The highlight of the professional basketball season for me was watching the NBA 50th Anniversary All-Star Game and the surrounding festivities at Cleveland's Gund Arena. It was a two-day affair, starting with the all-star practice on Saturday afternoon, and then that night, the rookie game, the three-point contest and the slam-dunk competition. The All-Star

Game itself followed on Sunday afternoon.

After watching Cincinnati beat Tulane in college basketball on Thursday night, February 6, I drove to Columbus, where I toured the state capitol, and then proceeded on to Cleveland for the weekend. The wind whipping off Lake Erie made it one of my coldest trips of the year. All of the events took place indoors, but on Saturday, the buzz of activity in downtown Cleveland was so intense, I couldn't find a cab after touring the Rock and Roll Hall of Fame. So in the icy wind, I wound up walking 10 blocks to Gund Arena. In addition to freezing half to death, I got scammed on a ticket, which we will discuss later.

During warm-ups for the rookie game, I went down behind one of the baskets to take a picture of Roy Rogers, the former Alabama star who was then playing for Vancouver. I was proud to see him selected for this prestigious game. As I was taking pictures, a man came up alongside me and started taking photos himself.

"Who's that standing talking to Roy Rogers," I asked the man.

"That's Travis Knight," he replied.

"Who the hell is Travis Knight?" I shot back.

"He's my son!"

"Oh!"

I was embarrassed. Travis, who was then playing for the Los Angeles Lakers, was from Utah and had played college ball at Connecticut. His father was a nice man and appeared to take no offense at my ignorance.

The rookie game, won by the east squad with Philadelphia 76ers star Allen Iverson as the MVP, was fun to watch, but the most thrilling event to me was the three-point contest, in which Steve Kerr of the Chicago Bulls dazzled the crowd with his long-range shooting. Koby Bryant of the Los Angeles Lakers captured the slam-dunk contest.

Watching the All-Star Game was exciting — especially MVP Glen Rice scoring a record 20 points in the third period, leading the Eastern Conference to a 132-120 victory — but I got more of a kick out of seeing the players selected as the top 50 stars in the 50-year history of the NBA being recognized at halftime. The group included Bob Pettit, Julius Erving, Magic Johnson, Oscar Roberson, Bob Cousy, Wilt Chamberlain, and Larry Bird. Amazingly, 49 were still living and 47 were present at the game. Only Jerry West and Shaquille O'Neal were absent. Pete Maravich, of course, died of a heart attack several years ago and was represented by his two sons: Josh and Jaeson, who is now a walk-on for the University of Alabama basketball team.

During the NBA playoffs, which last almost as long as the regular season, I saw games in New York, Chicago, Houston, Salt Lake City, and Atlanta.

In June, I found myself shuttling between Chicago for the NBA Finals, Omaha, Nebraska, for the College World Series, and Detroit for the Stanley Cup Finals. After the Bulls took a 1-0 lead in the finals over the Utah Jazz, I flew from Omaha to Chicago with Paul Hufham, Chris Nix and my nephew Monty Montgomery. Alabama was playing in the College World Series but was off the next day, which gave us a perfect opportunity to see Michael Jordan and the Bulls bid for their fifth NBA Championship.

Of all the athletes I witnessed throughout my fantasy year on the road, Michael Jordan stood out from the crowd. His celebrity transcends sports. He seems almost bigger than the game. But for all the hype surrounding Jordan, he never disappoints. His incredible athletic ability is a thing of beauty. The way he can take over a basketball game is something to behold; I was constantly amazed watching him dominate a court full of tremendously talented athletes.

After watching the Bulls stage a 97-85 victory over the Jazz to take a 2-0 lead in the best-of-seven series, we hustled over to Gibson's, a famed restaurant and lounge where sports and entertainment luminaries gather. I had been there before and wanted to give the boys a taste of a postgame celebration. Gibson's didn't disappoint. Not long after we settled into our seats, Bulls guard Ron Harper walked in, followed by Dennis Rodman. They were standing around talking and both Monty and Chris got a thrill by getting to speak to the two players.

A while later, I noticed a strange looking group at a table in the corner. People kept approaching them. "Who are those people," I asked Monty.

"Oh," he said excitedly. "Those are the Smashing Pumpkins!"

I thought they were a little strange looking, but I didn't think they looked like pumpkins. Monty informed me that was the name of their band. He said they are really popular. I felt a little foolish, but then again, if Bobby Bare had walked into the place, the kids wouldn't have known him from Johnny Cash.

The next week, with the Bulls leading 3-2 and needing a victory to clinch the championship, I met Louise, Ann, and her husband Jamie, along with John and Betty McMahon and their son Jamie, in Chicago to see another slice of history. The Bulls didn't disappoint. Jordan played an incredible game and won his fifth NBA Finals MVP award in leading Chicago to a 90-86 victory. Steve Kerr, who I had watched win the three-point contest during the all-star weekend, nailed the winning shot with five seconds remaining.

It was fun to see the whole celebration scene, punctuated by the confetti drifting from the rafters onto the court and the Chicago fans soaking up their moment at the summit of professional basketball. We knew we had seen one of the greatest teams in NBA history in the midst of a dominant run.

The only bad thing about the experience was that the Chicago police felt the need to block off much of the city from automobile traffic. Obviously fearing the possibility of rioting by jubilant Bulls fans, they had sealed off much of the downtown area. It took us a long time to find a cop who would let us through so we could get back to our hotel. But it was worth the wait to have seen the Bulls make history.

In the middle of the NCAA tournament, I decided to take a closer look at the flip side of college basketball. Unlike the major schools who attract national publicity and media scrutiny in their bid for an NCAA championship, the teams vying for the NAIA national title toil in relative obscurity. I have always wanted to experience the pinnacle of small college basketball, especially since teams from the state of Alabama often earn the right to play in the NAIA tournament. One Alabama team, Birmingham-Southern College, has captured two national championships in recent years under Coach Duane Reboul.

On March 18, I flew from Birmingham to Oklahoma City on my way to Tulsa and the NAIA tournament. Stopping in Oklahoma City allowed me to tour the capitol, and by chance, I came upon Governor Frank Keating standing in the lobby throwing bean bags against the wall. Somebody told me it had something to do with a science experiment. I introduced myself and discovered that he was a friend of Senator Jeff Sessions. They had both served as U.S. Attorneys. I decided not to press the governor on the bean bag issue.

While in Oklahoma City, I visited with my friend Brent Haygarth, the world-class doubles player from South Africa, his wife Monica and son Courtland. In addition to visiting the former site of the Alfred A. Murrah Building, the scene of an American tragedy, we traveled to Norman and toured the University of Oklahoma campus. Later that afternoon, I drove to Tulsa and checked into my hotel, not far from the campus of Oral Roberts University, host of the NAIA national tournament.

Over the next two days, I sat with the parents and friends of several of the Birmingham-Southern players as the Panthers won two close games and advanced to the final eight teams of the 32-team tournament. I had breakfast with Coach Reboul, who introduced me to several of his players. It was evident to me why Birmingham-Southern is always ranked among the finest liberal arts colleges in America under Dr. Neal Berte's direction.

Talking with those young men, and hearing Coach Reboul tell me about them, it was clear that they are students first and basketball players second. It was interesting to hear them talking about their plans for graduate school and studying abroad. Unfortunately, the day after I left, Birmingham-Southern lost by two points to No. 1 seed and eventual champion Life College of Marietta, Georgia.

The NAIA tourney is wall-to-wall basketball. The games started at 9 a.m. and ran until nearly midnight. I highly recommend the NAIA tournament for the basketball junkie.

In 1976, I met a lady named Paula Unruh, who was chairman of the GOP in Oklahoma. In the months leading up to my sports trip, Paula had been going through some photographs and came across a picture of the two of us with Jack Kemp from all those years ago. She sent me a copy and, I must say, we looked young and cute. After we exchanged notes, I told her about my trip, so when I arrived in Tulsa, Paula and her husband Jim were nice enough to take me on a tour of the city. They shared the history of Tulsa's oil barons while driving me through the neighborhoods where many of the beautiful old mansions reflect that golden era.

After watching dozens of basketball games at various levels of competition, I look back on my two days in Tulsa with a sense of wonder. Far from the maddening crowds and the media blitz, the players competing in the NAIA tournament represented a pure form of competition. The arena was half empty. There was no television. No one was headed for the NBA. Yet, with all the trappings of big-time college basketball stripped away, the players fought for the right to advance with as much intensity as the big names I watched claw their way to the NCAA Men's Final Four.

One of the most inspiring sporting events I experienced all year was the 49th National Wheelchair Basketball Championship at UAB's Bartow Arena in Birmingham. The dedication and perseverance of those athletes was amazing to watch. I never thought they would be playing such a physical game. At one point during the championship game, I saw one of the players knocked out of his chair. He struggled with all his strength to right himself and get back into the thick of the action. They played rough, tough, and were surprisingly good shots. I could not help contrasting that scene with some of the lethargic performances and attitudes I observed during the NBA season. It made me question the definition of a professional basketball player. All of those wheelchair athletes have my admiration. ■

December 26, 1996
Delta Counter at the Birmingham Airport
*On my way! Photo taken by an embarrassed Louise as other ticket
holders wait in line — probably thinking this is my very first flight . . .*

January 1, 1997
Pasadena, California
Outside the Rose Bowl
*Edgar enjoys the pre-game festivities.
The Crimson Tide wasn't there to play,
but I wore my Bama hat, anyway!*

January 4, 1997
Green Bay, Wisconsin
NFL Playoff game: Green Bay Pack-
ers vs San Francisco 49ers
*Edgar wearing the disappearing rainsuit
under the worst of weather conditions.*

January 4, 1997
Green Bay,
Wisconsin
*Edgar freezing to
death pre-game
where some fans
shared their
friend, Jim Beam,
to help ward off
frost bite.*

**January 29,
1997**
Durham, North
Carolina,
Cameron Indoor
Stadium —
Duke vs North
Carolina College
Basketball
*Edgar ready for
the game except
that he should
have brought ear
plugs!*

February 14, 1997
Nashville, Tennessee, US
Figure Skating Championship
*John Zimmerman of Homewood, Alaba-
ma, and his partner finish 3rd and qualify
for the World Championship. John (second
from the right) waving to the crowd!*

March 1, 1997
Anchorage, Alaska
*Edgar with Musher DeeDee Jonrowe
before his big ride!*

March 1, 1997
Anchorage, Alaska
Musher Bill Bass, Edgar and Ann before The Iditaride.

March 2, 1997
Starting Line of The Iditarod, Anchorage, Alaska — *"The Last Great Race"*

March 6, 1997
Memphis, Tennessee
SEC Basketball Tournament
Edgar with LSU and Mississippi State fans at the "annual" reunion. Left to right: "Cousin" Bill Weldon, Edgar, Mac and Barbara McMillan, Jenny Royer, Cornelia Weldon and Bob Royer.

March 15, 1997
Winston-Salem, NC, NCAA Regionals
North Carolina Basketball Fans Teddy and Bert Salem of Tampa, Florida, celebrating NC victory over Colorado allowing Dean Smith to break Adolph Rupp's record!

March 31, 1997
Indianapolis, Indiana, Plump's Last Shot
While in Indianapolis for the Final Four, Louise and Edgar had lunch at Plump's Last Shot, owned by Bobby Plump, whose famous basketball shot was brought to the screen in the movie "Hoosiers."

March 31, 1997
Indianapolis, Indiana, RCA Dome, Men's Final Four.
Left to right: Vicki Welden Montgomery, Dot Welden, Louise and Edgar.

May 3, 1997
The 144th Annual Kentucky Derby.
Carter Kennedy, who traveled with Edgar to several horse races, outside Churchill Downs for the "Run for the Roses."

May 3, 1997
Louisville, Kentucky
Clyde Anderson and Edgar at the Kentucky Derby.

May 17, 1997
Baltimore,
Maryland,
Pimlico Race
Track
*Edgar outside
the entrance to
Pimlico Race
Track before the
122nd running
of the Preakness
Stakes.*

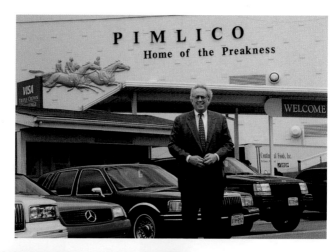

May 26, 1997
Indianapolis, IN
Indy 500
*Left to right: Doug
Thornton, David
Browder, Travis Pierce
and David Neill. Doug
Thornton's house —
where David, Travis
and David slept-over
after the race was
rained out.*

May 26, 1997
Indianapolis,
IN, Indy 500
*Edgar outside the
club room,
wearing Lou's
jacket, waiting
for those famous
words "Gentle-
men, start your
engines . . ."*

May 31, 1997
Birmingham Country Club
*Edgar and his "Main Man" Percy
Sledge at Ann and Jamie's wed-
ding reception.*

May 31, 1997
Birmingham Country Club
*Mr. and Mrs. Jamie Holman sharing their
first "toast" as husband and wife.*

June 2, 1997
Omaha, Nebraska
College World
Series, Rosenblatt
Stadium
*Left to right: Paul
Hufham, Edgar,
Robert Vaz (injured
Alabama player),
Monty Montgomery
and Chris Nix.*

June 7, 1997
Detroit, Michigan, Stanley Cup Finals
Edgar at Joe Louis Arena.

June 13, 1997
Chicago, Illinois, NBA Championship Game
— Chicago vs Utah
Jamie and Ann in front of the statue of Michael Jordan at the United Center.

June 22, 1997
San Diego, California Mariner's Point Park
Edgar and Jimmy LeVan, bike competitor at the X-Games, having an X-treme time!

June 28, 1997
Las Vegas,
Nevada,
MGM Grand
*Edgar at the
Holyfield-Tyson
Fight — smiling
before the sporting
event which was
to be a Champi-
onship bout but
was turned into a
street brawl by
Tyson's tactics.*

**August 23,
1997**
Williamsport,
Pennsylvania,
Little League
World Series
*Edgar standing on
the hillside at the
Little League
World Series
Championship
Game between
Mexico and the
USA.*

**August 23,
1997**
Williamsport,
Pennsylvania,
Little League
World Series
*Edgar standing in
front of the sign
with the past
champions —
Southside of
Birmingham,
1953.*

CHAPTER FOUR

"...He Couldn't Fix a Bicycle!"

My adventure through the ballparks and arenas of America started out as purely a sports quest, but the trip turned out to be about more than attending events. It was a way to use sports as a means to travel across the country, see interesting places, and meet people from all walks of life. If all I had done all year was go to games and watch the action on the field, ignoring the scenery and the people, it could have been a pretty boring year, like reducing every baseball game to a boxscore. The interesting people I met gave context to the trip, and in many cases reinforced my belief in the genuine decency of the American people.

All year long, I was often amazed at the way many of my new friends endured my incessant questions, went out of their way to help me and, in larger sense, participated in my trip. Many of them wanted to share my dream, and the way they embraced my trip enhanced the experience, leaving me with memories that will stay with me forever.

One of the most memorable characters I met was Doug Thornton.

Over a seven-day period during the middle of April, I traveled to a dozen different cities and saw 13 different sporting events. The week started in Gainesville, Florida, where I watched the NCAA Women's Gymnastics Championships with an old girlfriend from the fifth grade, Annette McCrory.

Annette was nervous because her only daughter Natalie, who had worked with our company while attending the University of Alabama, was expecting triplets. Two weeks later, she and her husband Hutch Brock would be the proud parents of two boys and a girl.

After leaving Gainesville, I went to Princeton, New Jersey, for a college tennis match; to New York for the NFL draft and a Stanley Cup playoff game between the New Jersey Devils and the Montreal Canadiens; to Providence, Rhode Island, for collegiate baseball, softball and lacrosse; to the Boston area for the U.S.-Mexico World Cup qualifying soccer match, a Red Sox-Orioles baseball game, and the Boston Marathon; to Hanover, New Hampshire, for a softball game; to Burlington, Vermont, for a college baseball game; and to Pittsburgh for the Pittsburgh Penguins-Philadelphia Flyers Stanley Cup playoff game, which would turn out to be Mario Lemieux's final home appearance.

Even though both my daughter Ann and my son Ed played soccer as children, I must admit I'm not very astute about the game. But Louise is! Many years ago, Louise and I saw our first soccer match when our son Ed played his first match on an organized team. Neither one of us knew anything about the game, but at the end of the match, when I was heading to the car, I looked back to see Louise giving the official hell about some of the calls he had made on our son!

The buildup for the U.S. vs. Mexico qualifying match in the World Cup was huge, and I was caught up in the hysteria. Instead of playing at the Rose Bowl, where they could have drawn more than 100,000 spectators, the U.S. side decided to host the match at Foxboro Stadium near Boston, which seats 62,000. You don't have to be a math genius to realize that the U.S. gave up in excess of $1.2 million for the privilege of protecting the home-field advantage. There was a fear that if the match had been held in Southern California, the stadium would have been filled with Mexico fans. However, in Foxboro, there were only about 4,000.

One aspect of soccer that makes it difficult for novices like me to appreciate is the sometimes long periods without scoring. But in this match, we had action almost immediately. One of the U.S. players kicked the ball into the head of one of his teammates and it bounced off him and into the opposing goal, giving Mexico a flukish 1-0 lead. The match ended in a 2-2 tie, which was like a victory for the underdog Americans, helping the U.S. team qualify for the World Cup.

The most memorable aspect of the whole day would turn out to be meeting Doug Thornton and his eight-year-old son, Clifford. The match was a hard sellout and I went to the stadium without a ticket, but determined to get in. After parking my rental car, I started walking toward the stadium holding a single finger in the air and periodically yelling, "I need one . . . " But I had no luck.

Eventually, about a quarter of a mile from the stadium, I came upon Doug and his son, who were standing under a tree. He was trying to sell an extra pair of tickets and I needed one ticket, so he waved me down. Doug was afraid to split the pair and I was afraid that I wouldn't be able to find a single, so I caved and bought the pair for face value of $40 each. Immediately, we walked to the stadium and the three of us sat in our four seats, which gave us a good view on the equivalent of the 20 yard line.

I was surprised to learn that Doug and his son live in Indianapolis, where Doug is an electrician and coaches his son's youth soccer team. They had driven all the way to Foxboro in their van, where they slept at night. I couldn't believe he would come all that way and sleep in a van at night just to see a soccer match. Like I had room to talk. He couldn't believe I would come all the way from Birmingham, especially since I wasn't that big of a soccer fan. Plus, he was curious about my year-long trip.

As we discussed my trip, he asked me if I was going to attend the Indianapolis 500 the next month. Of course I was. So he told me that he lived very close to the track and he would be happy to let me stay with him. Before we went our separate ways after the soccer match, I wrote down his name and telephone number, but the truth is, I never expected to see him again.

Two graduates of Mountain Brook High School, Patrick Sweeney and Julia Doster, were playing sports in the Ivy League, so I arranged my schedule to be able to see both of them play in April. I traveled to Princeton University to see Patrick play tennis and to Dartmouth College to see Julia play center-field on the softball team.

In high school, Patrick Sweeney was an honors student who had won the No. 1 singles tennis championship for the state of Alabama and had played on the basketball team. His father, Don, is a prominent Birmingham attorney and he and his wife Ann are friends of ours. In the late 1950s and early '60s, Don and his partner Ed Hatch were the three-time state high school doubles champions from Shades Valley High School. One of those years, they knocked off an outstanding team from Wetumpka High School in the first round, 6-0, 6-0. When I went to Princeton, Don and Ann were on campus for parents weekend, so I sat with them as Patrick won his doubles match against Dartmouth.

I have known Julia Doster since she was a barefoot toddler hanging around the little league field watching her two older brothers compete. Through the years, we watched her grow into a star softball and basketball player at Mountain Brook High School and a pretty young lady. Having known her all those years, it was an unusual feeling to show up on a beautiful spring afternoon in New England and watch her play centerfield. I thought she was the best player on the team, and I could under-stand why she was an All-Ivy League centerfielder. In my mind's eye, I could still see her playing on the same all-star team with my daughter Ann more than a decade earlier. The Dartmouth team lost both games to Princeton the day I was there, and knowing how competitive Julia has always been, I knew how tough it was to play on a team that was struggling that year.

During that week, I found myself in Providence and decided to place a telephone call to my daughter-in-law's grandparents. Danielle, who married my son Ed in 1995, was born to a couple who had met in the small west Alabama town of Livingston. Her father was a Yankee of Italian descent from Rhode Island who had come South to Livingston State University to play football. When Danielle was a little girl, her parents divorced and she lost touch with her paternal grandparents. They exchanged Christmas cards and such, but the grandparents had not seen her since she was a small child.

After locating their number and placing the call, I decided to have a little fun.

"Hello?" answered an elderly female voice.

"This is Edgar Welden from Birmingham, Alabama . . . "

"Who?"

"Edgar Welden. W-E-L-D-E-N. My son Ed is married to your granddaughter, Danielle Puccetti . . . "

"Oh, yes. Yes."

"Well, I'm down here at the Providence bus station and I'm out of money. I need to borrow bus fare home to Birmingham. Can you help me out?"

"Well, uh, uh, humm . . . "

You could tell she thought I was some nut, but I pressed on.

"I'll pay you back on payday."

"Well, uh . . . "

Unable to continue the gag, I finally broke down and told Rosalie that I was just joking and that I was in town for a sporting event and that Danielle had told me that her grandfather,

Gene, used to be a sportswriter for The Boston Globe. I told her I just wanted to introduce myself since we had never met. Rosalie apologized for their absence at the wedding; I had already known that her husband was in ill health and could not travel. We had a nice conversation and I told her that I would like to set a date to come back to Providence with Danielle and Ed, and she was delighted. She was warm and friendly and I could tell that she was pleased that I had called.

Five months later, when Louise and I traveled to New York with Ed and Danielle to the U.S. Open tennis tournament, we arranged a side trip to Providence and reunited my daughter-in-law with her grandparents. They welcomed us with open arms, treating us to a seven-course Italian dinner at the home of Danielle's Aunt Rosalie and Uncle Tony. We shared each other's company for several hours that night, telling stories and bonding for the first time, and I could see the joy in Danielle's eyes. That was one of the most satisfying evenings of the entire year, and it had nothing to do with sports.

In mid-May, as the Indianapolis 500 approached, I was confronted with a series of dilemmas. The race was scheduled for Sunday, May 25, six days before Ann's wedding the following Saturday. Also, the Alabama baseball team was selected to host a regional tournament and I was determined to see the Crimson Tide play. I thought they had a good chance of advancing to the College World Series, which has long been one of my favorite events. Unfortunately, the race, the pre-wedding activities and the baseball regionals presented some conflicts, so as the date of the Indy 500 approached, I was juggling several different scenarios of how to get there and how to get home. Adding to my problem was that the hotels in Indianapolis were requiring a three-night minimum.

After checking with the airlines, I finally decided to fly to Indianapolis on the day of the race and return that evening. Going with me would be David Neill, the 26-year-old son of our good friends Linda Sue and Jack Neill; David Browder, the 23-year-old son of our accountant O'Neal Browder; and Travis Pierce, my secretary's 13-year-old son. The two Davids had been extremely helpful in doing research for my trips.

In the weeks leading up to the race, we called Doug Thornton, the guy I had met at the soccer match in Foxboro, and asked if he would help us get back to the airport after the race. We would be catching an early evening flight and would need to hustle in order to make it. Doug was surprised to hear from me and happily agreed to help.

The week before the race, I traveled to the University of Alabama campus in Tuscaloosa, which is located 60 miles west of Birmingham, on three consecutive days to watch the NCAA South II Regional Baseball Tournament. Alabama defeated Troy State, Witchita State and North Carolina State to advance to the championship game against Southern Cal. The winner would advance to the College World Series. So now I had a dilemma: Should I go to Tuscaloosa on Sunday to see Alabama play for the right to go to Omaha, the pinnacle of college baseball, or to Indianapolis to see the world's ultimate auto race?

After some soul-searching, I decided to proceed with my original plans and go to Indianapolis. But on Saturday night I heard about impending rain for that area, so I kept a close watch on the weather. The next morning, I got up at 4:30 to go to the airport, fully intending to board the plane to Indianapolis. When I got to the airport and met the boys at the curbside baggage check-in area, I had a change of heart.

"Boys, I'm afraid it's gonna rain the race out and I'm not going," I said. "Y'all can go ahead if you want to, but I'm going to stay here and go to the baseball game."

So they decided to go to Indianapolis. I gave them Louise's cellular phone and Doug Thornton's telephone number and wished them luck. You should have seen the look on Karen's face.

That afternoon in Tuscaloosa, my friend Jay Stewart and I saw one of the most exciting college baseball games of the year. With two outs in the bottom of the tenth inning, 'Bama catcher Matt Fricke hit a home run to win the game, 9-8, and send the Crimson Tide to Omaha.

Meanwhile, in Indianapolis, the race was postponed because of rain.

After celebrating that exciting baseball victory, I called Karen at home to find out if she had heard anything from the boys. I knew she had been a little nervous about sending her 13-year-old only child off into the unknown. She told me that they had arrived safely, the race had been postponed to the following day and that the boys had wound up at Doug's house. So I asked Karen to call Doug and see if he could help them find a place to stay. After all, there were no hotel rooms available. Doug was very accommodating and offered to let the boys sleep on his living room floor.

Later I found out that Doug, a sandy-haired guy of medium build, takes the opportunity of the race each year to park cars in his yard and sell beer to race fans milling around his neighborhood. For three or four days during raceweek, his life revolves around the Indy 500, yet he never attends the race. He will stay around his house all day trying to make a little money, but he always walks over to the track, buys a souvenir and soaks up some of the atmosphere. However, when the NASCAR Winston Cup drivers descend on Indianapolis for the Brickyard 400, Doug buys a ticket and is there to see the action.

The rain actually allowed me to attend two coveted events. The next morning, I got up at 4:30 to catch the Delta flight to Atlanta and connecting to Indianapolis. If the flight arrived on time, I would get there about an hour before the race was scheduled to start, but the boys had my ticket with them, so I would have had to find Doug's house before going to the speedway. It was going to be close.

After changing planes in Atlanta, I found myself sitting in first class across from an average looking middle-aged guy in a coat and tie. Seated immediately in front of me were an attractive, well-dressed couple about my age. Across the aisle were a young couple. The two couples were talking as they took their seats, and it was obvious that they were together.

After pulling away from the gate, we took our place in line for takeoff. A few moments later, the pilot came over the intercom.

"Ladies and gentlemen, we have a mechanical problem and we're going to have to return to the gate . . . "

I started getting anxious. Even if we arrived on time, I was facing a very tight timetable to make the start of the race.

The man in front of me was obviously agitated and I realized then that he, too, was headed for the 500. "I told you we should have brought our plane," he said to his wife. "We're going to miss the start . . . "

About that time, the man seated across from me jumped out of his seat. "I'm a Delta mechanic," he shouted to nobody in particular as he headed for the cockpit. "Maybe I can help."

We were dumb-founded. It was as if Clark Kent had bolted out of the seat, exposed the big "S" on his chest and flown to the cockpit!

The man in front of me continued to moan and groan. At that point, I figured that my second chance at seeing the Indy 500 was slipping away. So, out of frustration, I blurted out, "That guy's from Birmingham and he's always doing this. He isn't really a mechanic and he couldn't fix a bicycle . . . "

The well-dressed man in front of me turned around and gave me a questionable look. I guess he wondered if I was serious.

A few minutes later, the man who had identified himself as a Delta mechanic walked back into the first class cabin and took his seat. I asked him what happened.

"I fixed the problem," he said nonchalantly.

I didn't know what to think, but a few minutes later, the pilot announced that the problem had been solved and we would soon be winging our way to Indianapolis. At that point, I wasn't sure I wanted to stay on that plane. But if the pilot was willing to trust the bicycle mechanic, I figured I would, too.

After we took off, I started talking to Lou, the man in front of me. He was heading for the race, and said he had flown up the previous day. Lou introduced me to his wife and his daughter and son-in-law, who were seated across the aisle. He said the main reason he was heading back was to take his son-in-law, who had never been to the Indy 500.

I told him I had never been to the race before and started asking him questions about getting to the track, since I was facing such a tight timeframe. Eventually, the subject turned to my year-long trip and he became extremely interested. Lou stood up in the aisle and called his son-in-law back to hear my story.

He then asked how I was getting to the track and where I was sitting. I had to tell him that I didn't have a clue. I told him that I was planning to take a taxi to the track and that I had to pick up my ticket at Doug Thornton's house.

"Who in the world is Doug Thornton?" he wanted to know.

"Well," I replied, "Doug Thornton is this guy from Indianapolis who I met at a soccer match in Foxboro . . . "

I could imagine Lou thinking — Doug Thornton? Soccer? Foxboro? — this poor guy will never make the start of the race.

Finally, Lou said, "Well, just come on and go with us . . . "

After we touched down in Indianapolis and taxied to the gate, we proceeded directly to the ground transportation area. Since no one was staying overnight, we didn't have to stop at baggage claim. When we walked outside, a black stretch limo was waiting and the five of us climbed in and headed for the track. Lou pulled out his cellular phone and called someone at the track.

"I need an extra ticket," he said to the person on the other end of the phone. "Meet us down at the elevator . . . "

As we sped toward the track, I could not believe my luck. Lou had made it quite clear that the best part of the race is the start, and I had boarded the plane in Atlanta worrying about how I was going to get to the track, find Doug's house and get to my seat in time to hear, "Gentlemen, start your engines!" Now I was heading to the race in style. My worries had melted away.

Several miles from the track, I saw people parking their cars and walking. Our limo pulled to within 30 yards of our gate and a nicely dressed gentleman met us, escorted us to the elevator and we all rode to a plush sky box. We had about 15 minutes before the start of the race, and I realized at that moment that if I had been forced to find Doug's house, I would have missed the start.

I didn't look like someone who had been invited to sit in a luxury box. After all, I had dressed casually, in khakis, a polo shirt and tennis shoes, anticipating a day out in the stands. My new best friend, Louis P. Ferrero, who looked like he stepped out of a Brooks Brothers catalog, took off his jacket so I would not be cold on this unusually cool, wet day as we lingered around the open-air area of the box. He introduced me to all his friends like I was really somebody.

"This is Edgar Welden from Birmingham, Alabama," he said again and again, "and he's taking a year off from his business to go see sporting events . . . "

I couldn't believe my good fortune. Good fun, good drink, good company and I made it to the race on time.

For the first time in 28 years, Jim Nabors, a native of Alabama, was not on hand for the traditional pre-race singing of "Back Home Again in Indiana." He had been in town on Sunday, but because of commitments in Hawaii, was forced to miss the second attempt of the race on Monday. Florence Henderson replaced Nabors, singing both the national anthem and "Back Home Again in Indiana."

As we awaited the start of the race, Lou put his arm around me and pointed toward Gasoline Alley.

"Now, Edgar," he said, "cars number 1 and 11 are ours . . . "

I knew the guy was connected, but I had no idea that he was an executive with a company that owned two Indy cars. It turned out that Lou is chairman and chief executive officer of Conseco Global Investments, an affiliate of Conseco, Inc., a diversified merchant banking concern, which provides capital and financing for companies world-wide.

Lou was right about the start. It was an amazing thing to watch. After Mary George announced, "Gentlemen, start your engines," the noise was incredible. I could feel the vibration reverberating throughout my entire body. The combination of the noise and the sense of raw mechanical power was overwhelming.

As I watched the beginning of the 81st running of the Indianapolis 500, I could not help appreciating the incredible history of the event. There's nothing quite like it in the world. Through the years, it has evolved into one of the signature sporting events on the planet and, at the same time, is perhaps the ultimate celebration of the combustion engine and all that the invention has spawned over the last century. Indianapolis is about speed and power and also about guts and daring and the desire to test the elements on a track where one wrong move can end in disaster.

In February, I had attended the Daytona 500, the most important event on the NASCAR Winston Cup circuit, and two weeks before Indianapolis, I had headed for the Winston 500 at Talladega, only to have it rained out. Auto racing has never held much appeal for me, even though the two races at Talladega Superspeedway generate more economic impact than any other sporting events in the state of Alabama and attract nearly twice as many fans as the storied Alabama-Auburn football game. On my travels around the country attending sporting events, I was constantly amazed at the incredible growth of the interest in NASCAR, which is no longer just a Southern sport. For instance, when I was in Pittsburgh for a bowling tournament, one of the children I met, Tim Pfiefer, was a huge NASCAR fan who wanted me to send him a NASCAR cap. Everywhere I went, I kept running into stock car racing fans, whether I was in New Hampshire, Michigan or California. I heard more about Jeff Gordon and Dale Earnhardt than I did about John Elway and Troy Aikman.

Both Daytona and Indianapolis were incredibly loud. The main difference was the machines. NASCAR is more accessible because they race with makes of cars that you can go to a showroom and buy (even though the street Taurus and the Winston Cup Taurus share, at best, a "remote ancestry") , while the Indy cars look more like rocket ships, which makes them seem more exotic.

After 15 laps at Indianapolis, it started raining again and the officials suspended the race. I didn't know how long the race would be postponed, so I thanked Lou and walked outside to see if I could find the boys. (When the race resumed on Tuesday, Arie Luyendyk would win his second Indy 500.) Luckily, I had written down the locations of our seats but when I went to those seats, they were empty. Then I pulled the cellular phone from my pocket and called Louise's phone, which I had given to David Browder.

"Hello," David answered.

"David! Where are you?"

"I'm at this pizza stand . . . "

And before he finished telling me exactly where he was, I looked to my right about 50 yards away and saw him. Considering that the track is more than 2.5 miles around, it seemed incredible to me that I could walk outside and find them so quickly.

"David," I said, "don't move . . . "

I told the boys that I thought they were going to postpone the race again and that we needed to go home. With the rain starting to intensify, we were standing outside the gates to the track, milling around tens of thousands of race fans looking for a way out, and then we looked up and an empty taxi cab appeared a few yards away. It was one of those days. Everything kept falling into our laps. We hopped into the cab, stopped at Doug Thornton's house to retrieve the boys' belongings, which gave me an opportunity to thank Doug for his incredible hospitality, and then proceeded to the airport to catch our flight to Atlanta, where we changed planes and headed to Birmingham. We were home in time for dinner. ■

CHAPTER FIVE

When a Man Loves His Daughter...

and Baseball . . . and Basketball . . .

and Horse Racing . . . and Hockey . . .

For the first five months of my sporting vacation, my friends kept teasing me, questioning whether I would be home for our daughter's wedding on May 31. Well, I know the suspense is killing you. I did make it. I was standing at the altar at St. Luke's Episcopal Church in Mountain Brook to give my daughter Ann away. At that moment, seeing the happiness in her eyes, I knew what it felt like to win the Super Bowl, the World Series, and the Final Four all in the same day.

The church was beautiful. Louise and Ann had planned a fantastic wedding. I was so proud and pleased that our families and friends had joined us for this very special occasion. We welcomed Jamie into the family. I wish Ann and Jamie a lifetime of love and happiness.

After the ceremony, we all headed to the Birmingham Country Club for the reception. Louise and I made our way into the ballroom and greeted family and friends. Then I spotted him out of the corner of my eye.

"Percy, my main man!" I exclaimed as I approached the bandstand, where Percy Sledge and his band were getting ready to perform.

Thanks to the chance encounter on the flight from Los Angeles to New Orleans for the Sugar Bowl in January, I had been able to engage Percy to sing at Ann's wedding reception. Just like I had said I would. Nothing to it.

A short time later, the bride and groom started dancing to "When a Man Loves a Woman," and a good time was had by all.

To be totally honest, having Percy Sledge sing was not Ann's idea. I'm not sure half of Ann's friends knew who Percy Sledge was. (In order to make everybody happy, we also had a band favored by the young people.) We knew Percy would be a big hit with our contemporaries, but to our surprise, Percy, my main man, really connected with the kids. As he was trying to leave the club, they crowded around him and didn't want to let him leave. Later, we took him back to the Mountain Brook Inn, where he was staying, and asked him if he would mind singing a song in the lounge. Well, he was very obliging and wound up joining our house band to sing three songs in the Rendezvous Room lounge. All those locals were amazed to be dancing to the vocal styling of the one and only Percy Sledge!

For all the planning that went into the wedding to prevent it from conflicting with anything of significance, it turned out that the University of Alabama baseball team had advanced to the College World Series and played its first game that same night. Like many of the men at the reception, I made my way from the ballroom to the men's grill to catch the final few innings of the Alabama-Mississippi State game on ESPN. After the Crimson Tide scored in the bottom of the ninth to sink the Bulldogs 3-2, the lounge erupted in cheers.

My year-long trip was well-known to most everyone at the reception, so someone asked whether I was going to Omaha.

"I'm heading out Monday morning," I said excitedly. "Who wants to go with me?"

David Hufham, a groomsman in the wedding, was standing next to his father, Paul.

"Dad," David said, "why don't you go?"

"Oh," Paul replied, "I can't do that . . . "

I wasn't surprised he said no. We had just met.

Sensing his reluctance, I assured Paul that I was serious. I told him that I had already planned to leave Monday morning and travel to Omaha with my nephew, Monty Montgomery. I told him that I thought he would have no trouble getting a flight and that I would check on it for him.

After David and his brother-in-law, Dr. Cal Dodson, convinced him to take me up on my offer, Dr. Paul Hufham decided to join me on one leg of my adventure. Paul, a retired Dothan dentist, had planned to drive home the next day with his wife Jean. But instead, he sent her back to Dothan, bought some clothes for the trip and caught the Monday morning flight to Omaha with me.

I had pulled yet another fan into my year of madness.

After Jim Wells took over the Alabama baseball program in 1995 and immediately turned the Crimson Tide into a national power, I started following the sport with renewed enthusiasm. In 1996, when 'Bama returned to the College World Series for the first time since '83, John McMahon, Frank Nix, Jim Jackson, Ed Finch, Tuffy Rainey, Lynne Keller (whose parents live in Nebraska) and I traveled to Omaha. Alabama was eliminated after three games, but I was hooked by the experience.

The College World Series is now one of my favorite sporting events. The city works hard to make the event special, and even though ESPN has helped build the CWS into a nationally recognized tournament, it has managed to retain a true amateur feel. Omaha's Rosenblatt Stadium is the home of the Omaha Royals Triple A team and is an excellent place to watch a game. As we have discussed previously, tournaments are near and dear to my heart and the eight-team double elimination format employed in Omaha makes for an exciting week.

I think all college sports should be run like college baseball. In most cases, major college football and basketball players go to college in order to enhance their professional sports prospects and, in many cases, place a limited emphasis on getting an education. In contrast, the best baseball players coming out of high school tend to sign with the pros and immediately start slogging their way through the minors. Thus, major league baseball pays for the training of its future players. The mandates of economics and talent typically push the less talented to college baseball, where they are forced to be true student-athletes and are prohibited from jumping to the pros until after their junior year.

After attending the CWS for the first time the previous year, I headed to Omaha on Monday, June 2, 1997, with great anticipation. Paul, Monty and I met Chris Nix, Frank Nix's son, at The Red Lion Hotel in downtown Omaha. Chris had been in Omaha for the early games and had arranged tickets for all of us, so we headed for Rosenblatt Stadium.

By the time we got to town, No. 1 seed Alabama had already beaten Mississippi State and Miami had defeated UCLA, setting up a second round game between the Crimson Tide and the Hurricanes on Monday afternoon. For the second year in a row, Miami handed Alabama its first defeat of the tournament, 6-1. In the second game, Mississippi State eliminated UCLA, which set up a Tuesday night elimination game between the Tide and Bulldogs.

On Tuesday morning, the four of us drove 60 miles to Lincoln, Nebraska, to tour the University of Nebraska and the state capitol. Later in the day, we returned to watch Stanford knock Auburn out of the tournament and then Alabama eliminate Mississippi State. At that point, we knew that 'Bama would be off on Wednesday and play again on Thursday.

Throughout the year, in my zeal to see a wide variety of sporting events, I was forced to juggle my schedule on an almost daily basis. Inevitably, one sport ran into another, which meant I had to make difficult choices and navigate through a maze of ticket, airline and hotel problems. The week after Ann's wedding would prove to be one of the most challenging periods of the year.

While we were enjoying the College World Series in Omaha, not only did we have to be prepared that Alabama could lose and send us home, I also was concerned about seeing the second game of the NBA Finals, the fourth and perhaps final game of the Stanley Cup Finals, and the Belmont Stakes, the final leg of horse racing's triple crown. All in a four-day period.

The one constant that week was the Belmont Stakes. The other events depended on several variables, but there was definitely going to be a horse race at the famed track near New York City on Saturday afternoon. My friend Carter Kennedy and I had attended the Kentucky Derby and the Preakness, so I was anxious to see if Silver Charm could become the first three-year-old since Affirmed in 1978 to capture the triple crown.

Back in May, Carter and I had spent one Friday afternoon watching the Bruno's Classic at Greystone Country Club in Birmingham and then flown to Louisville, Kentucky, to see the 124th Run for the Roses at Churchill Downs. I had been to the Derby before, and there's nothing quite like it. The ultimate horse race is awash in as much history and tradition as any sporting event in the world. In Kentucky, the Derby is as much a cultural milepost as a sporting event, at once linking the state's gentry to its rich heritage in thoroughbred racing and giving fans of all types an excuse to revel in the ultimate party. The ornate grandstand and the manicured grounds are filled with people from all walks of life, and elbow room is at a premium.

After betting on Silver Charm and winning several hundred dollars, Carter and I decided to make a quick exit. We were in a hurry to get to the airport, so after standing in line for a few minutes waiting for the pay-off window to open, Carter and I decided we should leave and find a cab or we would miss our plane. So I turned around and shocked the guy behind me by handing him my winning ticket and a business card.

"Hey," I said, "we can't wait. We've got to go catch a flight. This is a winning ticket. Would you cash it for me, keep $50 for yourself and send me the rest?"

He glared at me like I was crazy as we went rushing off. That was not a virgin look for me.

Several weeks later, after giving up on ever seeing any of that money, I received my winnings and a nice note from Michael Yaeger, who is senior vice president of marketing for Sutter Home Wine. He didn't even keep $50 for himself.

While in Omaha, I planned to combine a trip to the Belmont Stakes with a side trek to the Stanley Cup Finals. If everything worked out as I expected, I would fly to New York after the baseball tournament, see the Belmont and then ride the train to Philadelphia for the fifth game of the Stanley Cup between the Flyers and the Detroit Red Wings.

On Tuesday night, since Alabama was off on Wednesday, we decided to fly to Chicago the next day to see the second game of the NBA Finals between the Bulls and the Utah Jazz. Before watching the Bulls take a 2-0 lead in the best-of-seven series, we toured Soldier Field and Northwestern University in suburban Evanston. The boys also wanted to see Wrigley Field, so even though the Cubs were not playing that day, we stopped by for them to see the legendary facility. On Thursday morning, I assembled my group and flew back to Omaha, where we saw Alabama finally defeat Miami, 8-6, and set up a rematch for the next day.

One of the Birmingham television stations had a sports crew in Omaha and somehow got wind of our sports odyssey and interviewed Chris and Monty for the evening news. When they got back to Birmingham, they felt like celebrities.

After finding out Friday morning that the Red Wings had gone up 3-0 in the best-of-seven series and could clinch the Cup on Saturday night in Detroit, I faced a new dilemma. I still wanted to go to the Belmont and at that point, because Alabama was still alive in the tournament, I canceled my Friday flight to New York and rescheduled for Saturday morning. Since it was possible that the series might never return to Philadelphia, I now needed to get to Detroit. I found two flights out of New York, one out of Kennedy and another out of LaGuardia, that, while tight, would get me to Detroit in time to see at least part of the game following the Belmont. My last option, which I never expected to have to deal with, revolved around the possibility of Alabama beating Miami for a second straight day and advancing to the championship of the College World Series on Saturday. If Alabama advanced, I would be forced to choose between seeing the Tide play for a title and going to the Belmont. If I chose to stay in Omaha and root for 'Bama, then I would have to try to find a way to get to Detroit in time for the fourth game of the Stanley Cup Finals.

One of my group commented that the stock of several airlines plummeted when I started canceling all those reservations!

At this point, the travel agents were ready to throw up their hands. I could hardly blame them. I was embarrassed to call them anymore. I had concocted this master plan and even I was starting to get confused.

Not only did the Red Wings complicate my plans, but so did my own school. On Friday, Alabama knocked off Miami for the second day in a row, setting up a one-game championship show-down for Saturday afternoon against LSU.

Now I had to make a choice. Well, it wasn't much of a dilemma. As historic as it would have been to see Silver Charm win the triple crown, I knew that I could not have lived with myself if Alabama had won the national championship without me. Numerous times throughout the year, I faced difficult conflicts, but the choices become easier when you have a rooting interest or loyalty to one of the participants.

Late Friday night, I canceled my flights from Omaha to New York and New York to Detroit. I already had a reservation from Omaha to Detroit, so I booked a flight from Detroit to Birming-ham for Sunday, so I could be back in time to see Ann and Jamie return from their honeymoon.

As we headed from our hotel to Saturday's championship game of the College World Series, I couldn't help reflecting on our wonderful week in Omaha. Even though Paul and I had not met until my daughter's wedding the previous week, we had tempted fate and spent six straight days together and had enjoyed each other's company immensely. Our similar back-grounds and common interests had given us plenty to talk about and our fellowship with the boys made for a fun-filled week.

We pulled into the same parking place a block from the sta-dium. One of the great things about the College World Series experience is the incredible hospitality of the people in Omaha. Paul had befriended a home owner near the stadium, and he saved us a parking place in his front yard for every day that Alabama played. Then we walked across the street to a tiny souvenir shop, which is owned by a local attorney and open only during the week of the CWS. Every game, we stopped by the shop and visited with the owner and other fans.

One day while in the shop, I met a young man named Kris Boltin, who was a college student interning for the summer with the Omaha Royals minor league baseball team. On Saturday, I told Kris about my tight connection to get to Detroit and he volunteered to drive me to the airport. Kris collects sports programs and as a thank-you for his help, I sent him several programs from my trip.

Unfortunately, Alabama's luck ran out in the finals. LSU scored nine runs in the first two innings and coasted to a 13-6 win to clinch the national championship. In the middle of the eighth inning, realizing that the Crimson Tide was doomed, I dashed out of the stadium and met Kris, who rushed me to the airport to catch my flight to Detroit.

After seeing several hockey playoff games, including stops in Boston, Tampa, New Jersey, Pittsburgh, and Philadelphia, I was determined to see the winners skating around the ice with that big cup held over their heads.

Even though I had no exposure to hockey growing up, I had become a fan of the sport during the 1970s, when the now defunct World Hockey Association's Birmingham Bulls franchise captivated the Magic City. I was fortunate to have been in the stands the night Gordie Howe scored his 1,000th professional goal against the Bulls at the Birmingham-Jefferson Civic Center in 1977. Wayne Gretzky, regarded by many as the greatest hockey player of all time, skated on the ice at the Birmingham arena as a 17-year-old phenom for the Indianapolis Checkers.

In those days, my son Ed and I attended numerous Bulls games. Ed was big and athletic and played pee wee football, basketball, baseball, tennis, and soccer.

A friend of ours, Jay Rainer, recruited Ed to join their youth hockey team, but Ed was new to skating and had trouble stopping. The only way he could stop was to hit the rail and bound into the stands. So they made him the goalie.

All of this personal history with hockey was bouncing around in my head as I rode to Joe Lewis Arena in downtown Detroit. Luckily, I got there before the game started and had time to purchase some souvenirs. Figuring the Red Wings would clinch the Cup, I wanted to beat the rush to the souvenirs. And besides, knowing the history of Detroit and fearing that the impending celebration would get out of hand, I was determined to get the hell out of there as soon as possible.

After waiting 41 years to win the Stanley Cup, the Detroit fans were pumped to a fever pitch. During my travels, I discovered that hockey fans are probably the most emotional of all sports fans. The game is extremely fast-paced and physical, and the fans sit so close to the action they feel as if they are in the rink. You can hear the bumps and grunts and you can feel the collision of players, especially when they slam each other into the plexiglass surrounding the rink. At Joe Lewis Arena, most of the Detroit fans were wearing Red Wing jerseys with the name of their favorite player on the back. They were serious and intense. You didn't see many smiles in the crowd.

After I finished purchasing my souvenirs, I heard a tremendous roar in the distance. I rushed inside the arena and looked up at the matrix board dangling above the ice to see pictures of two older gentlemen in suits. I thought perhaps they were the owners of the team, so I turned to one of the two police officers standing next to me near the portal.

"Who is that?" I asked, pointing to the scoreboard, trying to yell over the noise of the crowd.

The big burly cop looked at me like I was from Mars. Dressed in khakis and a polo shirt, and clutching a shopping bag full of souvenirs in each hand, I must have looked like a K-mart shopper fresh from a blue light special.

"You don't know who that is?"

"No. Who?" I said sheepishly.

"Well," he said angrily, "if you don't know who that is, get the hell out of here!"

The second cop then looked me over with a contemptuous expression.

"Where are you from, anyway," he demanded to know.

"Alabama!" I shouted with pride.

Now I was mad.

"Let me ask you something," I shouted to both of the cops. "Do you know who Jay Barker is?"

They shook their heads no.

"Well, OK then . . . "

Later, I found out that the two men on the matrix board were two of the most famed players in Detroit Red Wings history, Ted Lindsay and Gordie Howe.

They had been members of the last Detroit team to win the Stanley Cup in 1955.

After finding my seat behind one of the goals about 30 rows up, I saw an exciting finish to the hockey season. Detroit won a 2-1 victory to clinch the Stanley Cup four games to none. The noise during the game was tremendous, and intensified as the fans could smell their elusive title. I was thrilled to see the Detroit players take turns skating around the rink holding the famed Stanley Cup aloft.

When I left the arena that night, I knew I would never forget the hallowed place Gordie Howe and Ted Lindsay occupy in Red Wings history.

But those two cops still don't know who Jay Barker is. ■

CHAPTER SIX

The Year of the Stadium Dog

I n the carefree days of my youth, the Major League Baseball ball-parks were shrouded in mystery. They were all so far away. For me, they were nothing but a dream. Baseball had not expanded beyond the cities of the northeast and midwest in those days. I could close my eyes and imagine what the funky center field at the Polo Grounds looked like, but all those places seemed like they existed in another world. Television was still in its infancy, and many Saturdays throughout the summer, my buddies and I would crowd around our black-and-white set to watch the game-of-the-week hosted by Dizzy Dean. At that time, television's presentation of the sport remained somewhat primitive, so instead of eliminating the mystery of places like Yankee Stadium and Fenway Park, by offering us limited glimpses of all those magical places, television actually made them seem even more exotic.

In the mid-1950s, on a trip with my parents to Chicago and Milwaukee, I got to see games at both Wrigley Field and Milwaukee County Stadium, where it was a thrill to watch my heroes Eddie Mathews and Warren Spahn play for the old Milwaukee Braves. After I became an adult I was able to see an occasional big-league game, especially after the Braves moved to Atlanta in 1966.

My year-long adventure began with two goals. I wanted to see all the state capitols and all the Major League Baseball ballparks.

While I was crisscrossing the country in the constant pursuit of various sporting events, it took me from the first week in April until the last week in September to squeeze trips to all 28 Major League ballparks into my schedule. Some of the highlights of my baseball tour included the first major league inter-league game between the Texas Rangers and the San Francisco Giants; the 50th anniversary of Jackie Robinson breaking the color line at Shea Stadium in New York, in which Bud Selig, the acting commissioner, announced that Robinson's No. 42 jersey would be retired by every Major League ball club; and the opening of Turner Field in Atlanta. I also saw the final three games of the World Series and the All-Star Game.

This chapter will include my ratings of all the ballparks. (BankOne Ballpark, home of the Arizona Diamondbacks, and Tropicana Field, home of the Tampa Bay Devil Rays, hosted their first Major League games in 1998.) I make no pretense about employing any sort of scientific method in my madness. I made the trip as a fan, and to me, the journey was like a pilgrimage to the fields of my dreams. My ratings are purely subjective.

In my opinion, baseball should always be played outdoors and on natural grass. Because of this philosophy, I tend to view domed stadiums with a certain amount of contempt, which is not to say that all domed stadiums are bad. Some surprised me. However, in almost all cases, a poor open-air facility is more conducive to a good baseball experience than a terrific dome. So my ratings have been significantly affected by my disdain for indoor baseball. Also, in recent years, I have been disturbed by the trend of stadiums being renamed on behalf of corporations. The folks in Cincinnati may want to call the ballpark Cinergy Field, but it will always be Riverfront Stadium to me.

In no particular order, here are some of the factors I considered in rating the facilities:

- Location of park and accessibility by taxi to and from my hotel.
- Concession stands with TVs so you don't miss any of the action.
- Cleanliness and convenience of restrooms.
- Comfort of seats (width and leg room).
- Proximity of seats to the playing field.
- Freedom and ease of movement within the stadium.
- Sophistication of electronic scoreboard.
- Presence of cup-holders on back of seat.
- Character of the ballpark.
- Quality and accessibility of food.

WELDEN'S RATINGS

No. 1: Wrigley Field, Chicago

I loved the ancient home of the Chicago Cubs. Wrigley Field, which was built in 1914 and seats approximately 38,900, was by far my favorite ballpark of the entire tour. I had a great seat two rows up behind home plate when I saw an inter-league game between the Cubs and the Milwaukee Brewers. The ambiance of the facility was unmatched, from the proximity of the seats to the field, which made you feel like you were part of the game, to the picturesque ivy-covered brick outfield wall and the fans sitting in lawn chairs atop nearby apartment buildings.

Ticket prices: $9 to $21.

Hot dog: $2.75.

Beer: $3.50.

Small soft drink: $2.50.

No. 2: Fenway Park, Boston

A close second in the Welden rankings, Fenway Park struck me as resembling one gigantic outdoor cocktail party. Everyone seemed to be having a good time, including me. Fenway opened in 1912 and seats approximately 34,200. I sat about 20 rows up between home plate and first base to see the Red Sox play the Baltimore Orioles. Eventually I started talking to several of the people around me, including the guy directly behind me, who was from New Orleans. As we drank beer and enjoyed the game, I exchanged some good-natured North-South teasing with several Boston locals seated near me. The guy next to me was from California and was anxious to go see his sister finish the Boston Marathon later that afternoon. As I was leaving the stadium to go watch the end of the Marathon a couple of blocks away, I bought a hot dog and it was fantastic, easily the best I had all year. So I went back and bought another one.

Ticket prices: $10 to $30.

Hot dog: $2.25.

Beer: $4.00.

Small soft drink: $2.25.

No. 3: Camden Yards, Baltimore

I found the first of the new generation/old-look ballparks, which opened in 1992 and seats approximately 48,200, beautiful, spacious and comfortable. I sat down the right-field line to see the Baltimore Orioles play the Cleveland Indians. I was surprised by the wide variety of shopping and eating choices available beyond center field, and I spent much of the game walking around and soaking up the atmosphere while watching the action. The old warehouse facing center field, near where Babe Ruth's father once had a tavern, gives the ballpark an urban feel which sets it apart from many of the multi-purpose facilities around the country. This park inspired Cleveland, Denver, and Atlanta to build similar facilities.

Ticket prices: $9 to $30.

Hot dog: $3.25.

Beer: $3.75.

Small soft drink: $2.75.

No. 4: Turner Field, Atlanta

The new home of the Atlanta Braves, which opened in 1997 and seats approximately 49,800, has many of the attributes of Camden Yards plus several modern entertainment features, including batting cages, video games, souvenir shops and the Braves museum. I was there with my friends Jack Neill and David Browder for opening night against the Chicago Cubs. We sat in the club level, which all of the new stadiums have, and were amazed when several people came up to us after we had already gotten into the stadium and tried to buy our stubs for souvenirs. I liked the comfort of the seats and the easy access to the concession stands.

Ticket prices: $5 to $30.

Hot dog: $2.50.

Beer: $4.50.

Small soft drink: $2.75.

No. 5: Jacobs Field, Cleveland

I enjoyed the home of the Cleveland Indians very much. The ballpark, which opened in 1994 and seats approximately 43,300, is very similar to both Turner Field and Camden Yards. I sat about 25 rows up between home and third and felt very close to the action. I became very familiar with Jacobs Field. I attended one regular season game, the mid-season All-Star Game and the fifth game of the World Series there. The location downtown next to Gund Arena is very convenient and within walking distance of many of the hotels. Much like Atlanta and Baltimore, Jacobs Field has a nice picnic area which adds to the casual, comfortable atmosphere.

Ticket prices: $6 to $26.

Hot dog: $2.00.

Beer: $4.00.

Small soft drink: $1.75.

No. 6: Coors Field, Denver

The new home of the Colorado Rockies, which opened in 1995 and seats approximately 50,200, shares many of the amenities of the other new generation facilities. Louise and I sat 12 rows up along the third-base line to see the Rockies play the New York Mets. Unfortunately, for reasons that you will read about in chapter seven, I didn't get a chance to roam around the concourse or to buy a hot dog. It was the only park on my tour where I failed to get a dog. However, I can recommend the quick acting paramedics.

Ticket prices: $4 to $30.

Hot dog: $2.50.

Beer: $4.50.

Small soft drink: $2.50.

No. 7: Arlington Stadium

Adjacent to Six Flags over Texas in the suburb of Arlington between Dallas and Fort Worth, the home of the Texas Rangers, which opened in 1994 and seats approximately 49,100, is a beautiful modern brick stadium. I sat about 25 rows up from third base. The seats down both lines are very close to the action. One of the most enjoyable features of the new stadiums (Camden Yard, Turner Field, Jacobs Field, Coors Field and Arlington Stadium) is your ability to move freely throughout the stadiums. This free movement is encouraged so that patrons will utilize and enjoy the various food concessions and entertainment centers. It was unusual to see the modern office building abutting the outfield, where people could sit at their desks and watch the game. Before he ran for governor, George W. Bush, Jr. was the managing partner of the Rangers.

Ticket prices: $4 to $30.

Hot dog: $2.00.

Beer: $3.75.

Small soft drink: $2.00.

No. 8: New Comiskey Park, Chicago

Located on the blue collar south side of Chicago, the home of the White Sox, which opened in 1991 and seats approximately 44,300, is a notch below the rest of the modern facilities. Unlike Jacobs Field or Camden Yards, it does not have the quaint feel of a place designed to pay homage to the classic designs of an earlier era while providing the modern amenities. The New Comiskey lacks the open-air feel of the other new facilities. Lathrop Smith, a friend of my daughter, and I saw the White Sox play the Cincinnati Reds in an inter-league game . I visited the restaurant in right field. We sat behind first base.

Ticket prices: $10 to $22.

Hot dog: $2.00.

Beer: $3.75.

Small soft drink: $1.75.

No. 9: SkyDome, Toronto

One the most unusual venues in all of sports, the home of the Toronto Blue Jays, which opened in 1989 and seats approximately 50,500, is an indoor facility that combines many of the modern amenities with a retractable roof. I rented a room in the adjoining hotel which looks out over the outfield and enjoyed the luxury of sitting on my balcony and watching the game. Several years ago, TV cameras caught a couple of enthusiastic fans engaging in a different "sport" inside one of those hotel rooms during a game. I especially enjoyed the restaurant overlooking the field, Windows on SkyDome, which had a marvelous buffet and good wine. One tip: Reservations are recommended. Unlike all of the previous stadiums, SkyDome, for obvious reasons, has artificial turf.

All in Canadian dollars:

Ticket prices: $4 to $27.

Hot dog: $.99.

Beer: $3.21.

Small soft drink: $1.79.

No. 10: Kauffman Stadium, Kansas City

When it was built in 1973, the home of the Kansas City Royals, which seats approximately 40,600, bucked the trend of the era. Unlike Atlanta-Fulton County Stadium, Cincinnati's Riverfront Stadium, and various others, which were built for both football and baseball, Kauffman was designed strictly for baseball. I found it a very comfortable and pleasant place to see a game, with wide seats. A man-made waterfall runs down the embankment across the outfield. I sat 30 rows up behind home plate to see the Royals play the Milwaukee Brewers. While

Kansas City's facility graded high on comfort, I had to penalize it for surprisingly poor food. They didn't have any sauce or onions for the hot dogs.

Ticket prices: $6 to $15.

Hot dog: $1.75.

Beer: $4.00.

Small soft drink: $1.75.

No. 11: Busch Stadium, St. Louis

Outside the home of the St. Louis Cardinals stands a statue of my boyhood idol, Stan "The Man" Musial. I sat between third base and the left-field foul pole about halfway up to see the Cardinals play the San Diego Padres. Busch Stadium, which was built in 1966 and seats approximately 49,600, is one of the better multi-purpose facilities, although the proximity of the seats to the field is not nearly as close as the modern baseball-only parks. The restroom and concession facilities were just average. However, I was pleased to find a cup holder in front of my seat. Also, the Busch Stadium hot dog was terrific, ranking second only to the Fenway dog. They offered ample variety in condiments. As I was leaving the stadium, I stopped at the Musial statue to make a picture where I overheard a couple telling their five children how they had first met in front of The Man's bronze likeness.

Ticket prices: $7 to $23.

Hot dog: $1.75.

Beer: $4.25.

Small soft drink: $2.00

No. 12: Dodger Stadium, Los Angeles

Several months after the home of the Dodgers opened in 1962 with a seating capacity of approximately 56,000, Joe McInnes, Jimmy Massey and I were in California for a Circle K convention, representing the University of Alabama, when we all ventured to see the Dodgers. All these years later, I headed west to Chavez Ravine to see the Dodgers play the Colorado Rockies. The most impressive thing about this stadium to me was the modern Mitsubishi matrix board, which gave more detailed information about the players than any other stadium. I loved the Dodger hot dog, which ranked third behind Fenway and Busch. However, parking was a hassle, which cost Dodger Stadium points on the Welden scale. I had to take escalators from the parking level up to the stadium entrance.

Ticket prices: $6 to $14.

Hot dog: $3.00.

Beer: $5.00.

Small soft drink: $2.50.

No. 13: Yankee Stadium, New York

The House that Ruth built, which was constructed in 1923 and significantly renovated in 1976, seats approximately 57,500 and is one of the hallowed shrines of baseball. You can smell the history, from Babe Ruth to Joe DiMaggio to Reggie Jackson. However, it's in a lousy neighborhood, the South Bronx, and the food is poor. I sat in left field for a game against the Montreal Expos because some hustler lied to me about my ticket location.

I was extremely disappointed in the accessibility of concessions and restrooms as well as the corridor space within the stadium. The stadium looks old and worn.

Ticket prices: $7 to $45.

Hot dog: $3.25.

Beer: $5.25.

Small soft drink: $2.50.

No. 14: Qualcomm Stadium, San Diego

The home of the Padres, which was built in 1969 and seats approximately 67,500, was known until recently as Jack Murphy Stadium. It shares much in common with the facilities in Pittsburgh, St. Louis and Cincinnati. I felt somewhat isolated from the action on the field. I sat high up in the lower level behind home plate to see the Padres play the Colorado Rockies.

Ticket prices: $5 to $18.

Hot dog: $2.00.

Beer: $4.25.

Small soft drink: $2.75.

No. 15: Veterans Stadium, Philadelphia

The home of the Phillies, which was built in 1971 and seats approximately 62,350, is said to have the largest capacity in the National League. Unfortunately, the size of the multi-purpose stadium makes some seating isolated from the action. I sat about 30 rows up behind third base to see the Phillies play the Houston Astros. But there is good parking, easy accessibility, and a friendly staff. I found the hot dogs small and plain.

Ticket prices: $6 to $20.

Hot dog: $3.00.

Beer: $5.00.

Small soft drink: $4.00.

No. 16: Hubert H. Humphrey Metrodome, Minneapolis

The home of the Twins, located in downtown Minneapolis, which was built in 1982 and seats approximately 55,850, was my second favorite dome. I was pleasantly surprised. Even though I prefer open-air stadiums with natural grass, I enjoyed my experience while sitting 25 rows up behind home plate to see the Twins play the Kansas City Royals. It was clean and well-lit and the staff was extremely friendly. Concession facilities were good and they had TVs situated throughout the concourse, which meant I didn't have to miss any of the action.

Ticket prices: $4 to $19.

Hot dog: $2.50.

Beer: $4.00.

Small soft drink: $2.50.

No. 17: Tiger Stadium, Detroit

Built in 1912, the ancient home of the Detroit Tigers seats approximately 52,400 and is uncomfortable and void of most of the modern amenities. However, it has that wonderful old-time baseball feeling, like Fenway and Wrigley. The concession lines were extremely long and the hot dogs were just average, although they had a good selection of condiments. On the last week of the season, I sat with Louise and John and Caroline Abele in left field to see the Tigers play the New York Yankees. A new stadium is on the way. It can't come fast enough.

Ticket price: $4 to $20.

Hot dog: $2.50.

Beer: $4.50.

Small soft drink: $2.00.

No. 18: Three Rivers Stadium, Pittsburgh

Another of the multi-purpose stadiums, the home of the Pirates was built in 1970 and seats approximately 47,950. I sat behind home plate to watch the Pirates play the Atlanta Braves. It was easy to get in and out of the stadium and the food was good with plenty of choices. Three Rivers was one of the few stadiums with cup holders, which meant I had a place to rest my beer. However, the place had very little personality and the seating was significantly removed from the field, which did not allow me to feel close to the action. I sat next to Ray Billott, a Pirates season ticket holder and father of three, and his 7-year-old daughter Lauren. She was full of personality and interest in the ball game. We later became pen pals. (*See opposite page.*)

Ticket prices: $5 to $17.

Hot dog: $3.00.

Beer: $4.00.

Small soft drink: $2.00.

Thank you so much for sending the picture. I injoyed looking at them. The Baseball game was funner then I thout it would be. Insince you came. I hope you had fun exploring around the world! I am seven ~~years~~ years old and in →

second grade don't forget, I know your not in a grade I bet your already Married! And have children! Well as you can see I'm of course not Married, I don't even have a boyfriend! Exept for Rockys, Garrett, Mark, Esra, ~~~~ Well let me get on with it. OK, OK, you can I'd mide it I have seven boyfriends! Well there just friends, Sorry It was so late for me to send these, Your friend Lauren.

No. 19: Cinergy Field, Cincinnati

The home of the Cincinnati Reds, which opened in 1970 and seats approximately 52,950, is very similar to the stadiums in Pittsburgh and St. Louis. The round shape prevalent in the architecture of the late 1960s made this work for football as well as baseball, but also makes many of the seats for baseball removed from the action. I walked up to the ticket counter as the Reds-St. Louis Cardinals game was just starting and bought a ticket seven rows up behind home plate for $14. The stadium is fan friendly, with comfortable seating and average food. The stadium was within walking distance of my hotel.

Ticket prices: $3 to $14.

Hot dog: $1.50.

Beer: $3.75.

Small soft drink: $1.75.

No. 20: Pro Players Stadium, Miami

Originally built for the NFL Dolphins, the home of the Florida Marlins became a Major League facility as well in 1993 and seats approximately 47,650 for baseball. I sat behind home plate about 15 rows up to see the eventual World Champion Marlins play the Cincinnati Reds. The seats were comfortable and the concession and restroom facilities were adequate; however, the food was mediocre and I still felt like I was in a football stadium.

Ticket prices: $2 to $45.

Hot dog: $2.25.

Beer: $4.50.

Small soft drink: $2.25.

No. 21: Edison International Field, Anaheim

After the Los Angeles Rams fled to St. Louis, the owners of the Anaheim Angels converted multi-purpose Anaheim Stadium into a baseball-only facility. Originally opened in 1966 the reconfigured park now seats approximately 33,800. I sat along the third base line in the upper deck to see the Angels play the Oakland Athletics. I found the stadium lacking, despite the renovation.

Ticket prices: $4 to $38.

Hot dog: $2.75.

Beer: $5.00.

Small soft drink: $2.75.

No. 22: Shea Stadium, New York

The home of the Mets, which was built in 1964 and seats approximately 55,600, is difficult to reach and is average at best in everything. Years ago, it was the home of the NFL Jets as well, but it's worth noting that the stadium was so inadequate that the Jets moved to New Jersey, while the Mets had nowhere to go. I sat about 30 rows up between home plate and third base to see the Mets play the Dodgers in a game that commemorated Jackie Robinson's career.

Ticket prices: $9 to $35.

Hot dog: $3.50.

Beer: $5.25.

Small soft drink: $3.25.

No. 23: 3Com Park, San Francisco

The former Candlestick Park, which opened in 1960 and seats approximately 58,000, is the windiest facility in the Major Leagues. I sat in some temporary bleachers adjacent to the third base dugout to see the Giants play the San Diego Padres. The food and facilities were just average, although the lines to the concessions and restrooms were short because there were only about 10,000 people in the stands. I sat next to Richard Bernham, a Giants season ticket holder who only attends the daytime games, because it gets too cold at night, even during the summer. Bernham is a retired professor of Irish literature whose wife Carol had just written a book called "Attic Light."

Ticket prices: $5 to $24.

Hot dog: $3.00.

Beer: $4.00.

Small soft drink: $2.50.

No. 24: Astrodome, Houston

Once billed as the "eighth wonder of the world" when it was built in 1965 with a capacity of approximately 54,800, the home of the Astros was one of my least favorite venues of the year. The place was so big, I didn't feel like I was at a baseball game. I sat about 10 rows up between home plate and first base to see the Astros play the New York Mets. The stadium's accessibility to the rest of the city is poor and the food was mediocre.

Ticket prices: $5 to $23.

Hot dog: $2.00.

Beer: $3.00.

Small soft drink: $1.50.

No. 25: Milwaukee County Stadium, Milwaukee

Originally the home of the Braves and now of the Brewers, Milwaukee County Stadium was constructed in 1953 and seats approximately 53,200. I sat 15 rows up behind home plate to see the Brewers play the New York Yankees. I found it to be a run-down old stadium, very out-dated, with poor accessibility. There were few concession stands and the lines were long and slow. The good news is, a new stadium is under construction.

Ticket prices: $5 to $22.

Hot dog: $2.00.

Beer: $3.50.

Small soft drink: $1.75.

No. 26: UMAX Coliseum, Oakland

The home of the Oakland Athletics, which was built in 1966 and seats approximately 48,200, was the worst open-air stadium on my tour. It was very unattractive. The food and the facilities left much to be desired. I took the BART subway from San Francisco because I had been assured that the accessibility of automobile traffic across San Francisco Bay was unpredictable. When I walked out of the BART station and had to continue a long way over a fenced-in bridge to get to the stadium, I felt uneasy because there were so few people around. I sat about 12 rows up behind home plate to see the A's play the Texas Rangers.

On a positive note, I did get to see Mark McGwire hit a grand slam.

Ticket prices: $4 to $22.

Hot dog: $3.00.

Beer: $5.00.

Small soft drink: $2.00.

No. 27: Olympic Stadium, Montreal

Built for the 1976 Olympics, the home of the Expos, which seats approximately 43,700, was a disappointing venue. It took a 30-minute cab ride from the airport to see a dirty and poorly lit stadium with a retractable roof that didn't. I understand that since I was there the old roof has been replaced. I was concerned about getting a taxi after the game, so I convinced the cab driver, who had come to French-speaking Canada from Italy when he was six years old, to go to the game with me, and I bought him a ticket. We sat 12 rows up between home plate and third base to see the Expos play the Florida Marlins. I was especially disappointed in the little bitty hot dog and the poor choice of condiments, although like some of the new stadiums, in certain designated areas, they had a waitress take your order, which kept me from having to miss any of the action. I was surprised to see the messages on the scoreboard in both French and English. Later, someone told me it was the law.

All in Canadian dollars:

Ticket prices: $7 to $33.

Hot dog: $2.75.

Beer: $4.25.

Small soft drink: $2.50.

No. 28: Kingdome, Seattle

The home of the Mariners was my least favorite of all the Major League facilities. Opened in 1976, the Kingdome seats approximately 59,100. The upper sections of the Kingdome are very steep, making you feel as though you might slip and tumble off. You have to walk all the way up to your seats in the upper level on outside ramps. The corridors are very narrow. People walking through the corridors often must dodge others waiting in line for the concession stands. I sat in the upper level on the first base side to see an inter-league game between the Mariners and the San Francisco Giants. After the game, I was unable to get a cab so I caught a rickshaw-type bicycle to my hotel downtown. Too bad I didn't have one of those in some of the other cities where the traffic was so congested.

Ticket prices: $6 to $25.

Hot dog: $3.50.

Beer: $5.00.

Small soft drink: $3.00

Note: Thanks to the employees of the stadiums and concessionaires who provided the ticket prices, hot dog, beer and soft drink costs by telephone as I was writing this book.

During my travels, Major League Baseball confronted one of the biggest changes in the game since the advent of the designated hitter. For several years, the baseball establishment had debated the concept of inter-league play. Finally, in 1997, the American and National Leagues decided to have their teams compete against each other during the regular season.

Some traditionalists view inter-league play as just another gimmick, like the addition of the wildcard play-off team several years earlier. I'm one of those people who like the wildcard. It energizes the sport late in the season, giving the fans more to talk about than spitting and scratching. Also, I like the fact that no longer is one great second place team penalized for being in the wrong division and not getting a chance to play for the World Series.

Much like the change to the playoff structure and the addition of all the wonderful new ballparks, inter-league play has helped rejuvenate the fans who were turned off by the players' strike. It makes perfect sense for the Oakland Athletics and the San Francisco Giants to play each other. In fact, it's silly for them not to play. The same could be said for the Cubs playing the White Sox and the Yankees facing the Mets.

If you're going to play inside the house and on the carpet, you might as well offer your fans the opportunity to see Greg Maddux of the National League's Braves pitch to Cal Ripken of the American League's Orioles!

I was fortunate to see several inter-league games throughout the year, including the very first one of all time between the Texas Rangers and the San Francisco Giants. On June 12, I flew from Birmingham to Dallas/Fort Worth, where business associate Harry Clemens picked me up at the airport. After taking care of some business, we toured Texas Christian University in Fort Worth and Harry went with me to check into my hotel in Arlington. After having a quick drink, we walked to Arlington Stadium a couple of blocks away.

The historic nature of the event was reinforced by the presence of former Rangers pitcher Nolan Ryan and former Giants outfielder Willie Mays, who threw out the first two ceremonial pitches. Mays, the "Say, Hey!" kid, grew up in Fairfield, Alabama, and played for the Birmingham Black Barons as a teenager at Rickwood Field, which now is the oldest baseball stadium in the country. The presidents of both leagues were also on hand for the game, which San Francisco won, 4-3, before a crowd of 46,507.

The next day, I flew to Chicago to see the Milwaukee Brewers defeat the Chicago Cubs at Wrigley Field, 4-2. I sat behind home plate next to an attractive young lady who was dating Mark Loretta, the second baseman for the Brewers. They had met as undergrads at Northwestern, and Mark had always dreamed of playing in Wrigley Field. Until inter-league play, however, that dream seemed impossible, so while the traditionalists continued to debate the concept, I was confronted with a very positive result of the change. Since Milwaukee and Chicago are located only about 100 miles apart, the Brewers and Cubs are natural rivals who have been denied the chance to play each other all these years for arbitrary reasons.

When I was growing up in Wetumpka in the 1950s, I had to get up early every morning to deliver about 100 copies of The Montgomery Advertiser on my bicycle. After picking up the papers, and before embarking on my route, I would stop at Little Sam's Cafe, take a seat at the counter and read the sports page while eating a doughnut and drinking a cup of coffee. The thing I remember most about those days was checking the baseball standings to see how my St. Louis Cardinals were doing and the batting statistics to see where Stan Musial, my favorite player, ranked in relation to his archrival, Ted Williams.

In those days, kids looked up to baseball players as true heroes. I could never imagine Stan the Man doing anything wrong. Never in a million years would he have spat in an umpire's face, abused his wife, used illicit drugs or kicked a cameraman in the groin.

But the world is more complex these days. It's more difficult for kids to idolize athletes in light of the well-publicized failings of a few rotten apples. Because of greater media scrutiny, we know more about the athletes now than we did when I was young, and often, the things we learn disturb and sometimes shock us. Athletes have problems just like the rest of us, and when you look at their shortcomings, you're really observing nothing more than a mirror image of the society as a whole.

Sitting in Jacobs Field watching the 68th annual Baseball All-Star Game, I could not help being confronted by the realities of a world vastly different from the one of my youth. The case of Albert Belle struck me especially hard.

Belle had been an all-star outfielder for the Cleveland Indians before accepting a big money offer from the Chicago White Sox.

After Belle left, there was bad blood between him and the Cleveland organization, not to mention the Indians fans. Several weeks before the All-Star Game, he had been booed unmercifully by the crowd at Jacobs Field when the White Sox came to town. On the night when he was being honored by the fans for his talents and achievements, Belle acted like a spoiled brat by refusing to participate in the all-star group photo and then choosing not to play in the game. I found his behavior childish.

We know so much about the athletes nowadays and some incidents attract so much attention that they form an inaccurate impression. During the all-star festivities, while reading various newspaper articles, I began to think that Roberto Alomar had gotten a bit of a bad rap after spitting at an umpire the previous season. Of course, what he did was absolutely despicable. In no way do I condone such behavior. But after learning more about him and his family, the incident now appears to have been one random act of boorish behavior from an otherwise decent man.

Children growing up today are more cynical about their heroes and I think we all realize that it's risky to look to our favorite sports figures for more than great athletic performances. Now we seem surprised when great athletes like Mark McGwire, Sammy Sosa and Cal Ripken also turn out to be decent human beings who have class and are willing to assume responsibility for their undeniable status as role models.

When you strip everything away from my year on the road, it was defined by a thousand feats of incredible athletic skill. I found myself watching young men and women do things most of us can only dream about, in situations filled with pressure and various obstacles, and in that sense, I was watching them with the same wonder as I had during those carefree days in Wetumpka.

Like millions of fans watching on television, I could not help feeling a sense of joy for Indians catcher Sandy Alomar, who was named the MVP of the All-Star Game. In the seventh, with the game tied 1-1, Alomar slammed a two-run homer off Shawn Estes to key the American League's 3-1 win. Sandy, the brother of Roberto, had been on the Indians roster longer than any other player, and despite having earned the opportunity to become a free agent and chase the big bucks, he had decided to stay in Cleveland. The largely pro-Indians crowd gave him a rousing ovation. His story warmed my heart.

As I traveled around the major leagues, I soaked up the great performances like a sponge, storing up memories that will live with me forever. I saw Mark McGwire hit a grand slam one day in Oakland, not realizing that in 1998, he would break Roger Maris' single-season record for home runs. I marveled at the grace and consistency of San Diego Padres outfielder Tony Gwynn, the greatest hitter of the age. I took great pleasure in watching the incredible all-around abilities of Seattle Mariners star Ken Griffey, Jr. I watched in amazement as future Hall of Fame pitcher Roger Clemens shut down the Orioles en route to winning 21 games at the age of 35.

During the fall, at the same time that I was flying all over the country to watch college and professional football, I caught parts of both the American League Championship Series between Baltimore and Cleveland and the National League Championship Series between Atlanta and Florida. My children, Ann and Ed, are Braves fans and naturally, given the franchise's unrivaled success in the 1990s, they expected Atlanta to advance to the World Series. Even though I don't have a favorite team, I must admit, I was pulling for the Braves to make the Fall Classic because of Turner Field's proximity to Birmingham.

After watching the NFL's Washington Redskins win a Monday night game over the Dallas Cowboys at the new Jack Kent Cooke Stadium, I flew into Atlanta and met Ann, Jamie, and our friends Jim Jackson and Bill and Jean Wilson at Turner Field for game six of the NLCS. Marlins pitcher Kevin Brown, who had missed an earlier start because of an illness, was impressive in shutting down the Braves for a 7-4 complete game victory, ending Atlanta's two-year hold on the National League crown.

Based upon the regular-season standings, I felt sure that the Baltimore Orioles and the New York Yankees would play for the American League pennant. The Orioles had compiled the best record in the American League. In anticipation of a Baltimore-New York series, Louise and I had planned a two-city, four-night trip with friends from Alabama, Louise Reddoch and Morris Slingluff. Morris has family in Baltimore and loves the Orioles. Unfortunately, the Cleveland Indians knocked off the Yankees, and while we got to see the Indians play the Orioles in game two of the series at Camden Yards, we were already committed to travel to New York. The girls certainly didn't want to go to Cleveland, because Louise #1 and Louise #2 were determined to make sure that I fulfilled my commitment to take them to New York. Period.

End of discussion. Suddenly, I had no vote in my own adventure.

But we spent a wonderful day in Baltimore visiting with Morris' family and saw an outstanding baseball game. Our guide around Camden Yards and a source of endless information was Birmingham native Deak Nabers, who lives in Baltimore and was working on his second PhD at Johns Hopkins University. Many years before, when Deak was in the fourth grade, I had coached him on a baseball all-star team. He went on to become a Rhodes Scholar and is also one of the biggest and most knowledgeable sports fans I have ever met. Also joining us for the day were three friends who had driven over from Washington: Susan Stewart, her friend Gil Murdoch, and John Kennedy.

Early the next morning, the two Louises, Morris and I boarded a train for New York. Not until several days later did we discover that the Baltimore Sun had carried a front-page picture of Morris and his Louise reaching for a foul ball. What a treat for that life-long Orioles fan!

I skipped the start of the World Series between Cleveland and Florida to go to Hawaii to see the Ironman Triathalon. After returning to the mainland and watching on television as the Indians and the Marlins split the first four games, I found myself at Crestline Field in Mountain Brook on Wednesday, October 22 watching my son-in law Jamie Holman coach the fifth and sixth grade Packers against the Cowboys. I don't want to say who won, but the action was grueling. When it was all over, the field was strewn with blood, guts and heart.

The next day, I boarded a flight from Birmingham to Cleveland to catch game five of the World Series. It was my fourth trip to Cleveland in nine months. Let me tell you, visiting Cleveland four times in one year was not what I had in mind when I planned this trip. But in all seriousness, I enjoyed all four visits and was impressed with the way the city handled each event.

After watching the Marlins beat the Indians in Cleveland in game five and then seeing the Indians defeat the Marlins in Miami in game six, the nation's eyes turned to Pro Player Stadium for the seventh and deciding game on Sunday night. All my life I had dreamed of such a moment. In all of sports, few events can match the drama of a seventh game in the World Series. I was happy to share the experience with several friends from Birmingham who happened to be in the area the day of the game: John and Betty McMahon, Phillip McWane, Penny and Ruffner Page and Bill and Carey Hinds.

After a season on the road watching the best and worst the game had to offer, the season reached a perfect climax with the world championship on the line. I was pulling for Cleveland, but when career minor leaguer Craig Counsell of the Marlins hit a sacrifice fly into right field in the bottom of the ninth to send the game into extra innings, I could not help feeling like a part of history. The tension was incredible. Every pitch. Every swing of the bat. Every fielded ball. I wondered what it must feel like to confront such pressure. In the bottom of the 11th, when Florida shortstop Edgar Renteria slapped a bases-loaded single up the middle to give the Marlins a 3-2 win and the World Championship four games to three, part of me was a bit sad. Part of me wanted the drama to continue. Renteria's heroics ended more than his magical baseball season. It ended mine as well. ■

CHAPTER SEVEN

New York, Hell!

*I*n 1965, when a pretty Chi Omega from the University of Alabama
named Louise Cleve married me, she vowed to accept our union for
better or worse. But she never expected a day like August 15, 1997.

In the week leading up to our 32nd anniversary, August 14th,
my schedule was jam-packed with travel.

For years my friend Ray Scott, the founder of Bass Anglers
Sportsmans Society (B.A.S.S.), the bass fishing tournament
organization, had encouraged me to attend one of their events.
B.A.S.S. is headquartered in Montgomery. On Thursday, August
7, I took the opportunity to drive from my home in Birmingham
to the early-morning launch of the B.A.S.S. Masters tournament on Lake Logan Martin near Pell City. While standing next
to the pier, I ran into Trip Weldon from Wetumpka, a friend of
our family but no relation. He gave me a VIP ticket and a parking pass to the weigh-in later that afternoon at the Birmingham-
Jefferson Civic Center. After leaving the B.A.S.S. launch, I
drove to Tuscaloosa with my friend Jim Rice to the Paul Bryant
Museum for the dedication of the Bryant stamp being intro-

duced by the U.S. Postal Service. A large contingent of the coach's former players and protegés had gathered for the historic event. Later in the afternoon, I drove back to Birmingham for the B.A.S.S. weigh-in. Obviously, fishing is big in Alabama, but I was still amazed to see about 10,000 spectators in the stands from around the country at the Civic Center to see the competitors weigh their catch of the day.

The next morning, Louise and I headed west for what would be one of the most memorable trips of the year. Instead of packing this leg with wall-to-wall sporting events, I decided to combine the need to see a baseball game at Coors Field in Denver and my desire to tour the state capitols of Idaho, Wyoming, Montana, and Colorado with the celebration of our wedding anniversary by taking Louise to two of the most beautiful resort destinations in the entire country, Sun Valley, Idaho, and Jackson Hole, Wyoming. By squeezing in a side trip to Yellowstone National Park, we wound up celebrating our anniversary in, of all places, Cheyenne, Wyoming.

Although I had planned to take Louise out for a romantic dinner, we ended up at the Hitchin' Post Steakhouse at the Best Western, which I would generously describe as rustic, sitting next to a really nice couple whose RV had broken down earlier that day. We started talking to them and the next thing we knew, they had retreated to their motel room and brought their grandchildren back to entertain Louise on her special day, turning our romantic anniversary dinner into anything but. After a while, we returned to our "suite" at the Little American Inn, which was classified as a "suite" because it included gaudy

French brocade furniture, a big-screen TV, and a sheer curtain separating the bedroom area from the living room area. But Louise took it all in stride.

However, I may be paying for the next day for the rest of my life.

After checking out of the Little American Inn in Cheyenne on the morning of August 15, we started the day by touring the Wyoming state capitol. Then we drove our rental car across town to visit the Frontier Days Old Western Museum, which I found very interesting. Unfortunately, I had been unable to squeeze the annual Frontier Days Rodeo, which is held each July, into the trip. Our final destination that night would be Denver, where we would see the Colorado Rockies play the New York Mets, but the day would be packed full of adventure. On our way to Denver, we stopped in Fort Collins to tour the campus of Colorado State University and in Boulder to tour the University of Colorado.

After arriving in Denver that afternoon, Louise insisted that we stop by McNichols Arena, home of the Denver Nuggets of the NBA and the Avalanche of the NHL, to watch the men's all-around competition at the John Hancock U.S. Gymnastics Championships. Then it was downtown to tour the Colorado capitol and to check into our hotel, The Brown Palace, before heading over to Mile High Stadium, home of the Broncos. I knew Louise didn't want to miss the soccer match between the Colorado Rapids and the New York/New Jersey MetroStars.

What would an anniversary be without these exciting sporting events? My friends often accuse me of being a romantic fool.

After all those preliminaries, we arrived a little late for the Rockies-Mets baseball game, taking our seats about 12 rows up along the third base line. Later, Louise and I were planning to meet a friend from Wyoming, Tom Sansonetti, and his wife Kristi back at our hotel for dinner. In the bottom of the seventh inning, when Todd Helton came to bat for the Rockies, I decided to have a little fun, so I pulled out my cellular phone and placed a call to my friends John and Janice Clements back in Birmingham. John and I are always trying to stump each other with sports trivia questions.

"Hey, John," I said, "do you know who Todd Helton is?"

Before John could answer, Janice, who was on the other extension, chimed in, "Oh, yes, he used to play quarterback for Tennessee!"

Helton, recently called up from the minor league, who two years earlier had also been the MVP of the College World Series, slapped a base hit to left field. Then left-handed Larry Walker came to the plate, and since he was having a great year and contending for MVP honors, I decided to watch him bat before departing the stadium. On the first pitch, Walker slammed a line-drive foul ball right toward us. I cannot adequately describe the feeling of terror. It was like watching a missile heading straight for your head. Your first reaction is to raise your arms to protect your face, which both of us did. Unfortunately, the ball struck Louise on the right arm.

Louise grabbed her arm and it was clear that she was in

intense pain. "Edgar," she said, "I think it broke my arm . . . "

Our first reaction after the initial shock was to feel relieved. If the ball had hit Louise in the head with the same force, it could have been fatal. She was very lucky. Of course, at that moment, she didn't feel lucky. She wasn't as relieved as I was, since her arm was broken. The pain was excruciating and she started to feel faint, so I asked someone sitting behind us to go find some ice.

I wanted the ice not only to place on her arm to keep it from swelling but also to apply to her forehead, because Louise has a low threshold for pain and a tendency to faint. Louise has taken a certain amount of kidding from her children for several of her fainting spells through the years, such as the legendary time when she fainted in front of the frozen food section of a convenience store while on vacation in Sarasota, Florida.

As Louise drifted in and out of consciousness, the Coors Field paramedics appeared very quickly and wanted to escort us to the first-aid station.

"But she can't walk," I said. "She'll pass out."

"Well," one of the paramedics said, "we'll carry her."

So the paramedics picked up Louise, one holding her under the arms and the other by her legs. Later, Louise would remark, "I was glad I wasn't wearing a dress. The way they carried me out wasn't very ladylike."

As the paramedics carried her up the steps to the next portal, the crowd gave her a standing ovation, just like they would an injured player. I trailed behind them, with her purse in one hand and my camera in the other. Since I had been diligent about documenting my entire trip, I wanted to take a picture of Louise being hauled up those steps. It was a pretty funny sight. But I was afraid if I took her picture in that condition, the fans would rush me.

Shortly after we got to the first-aid room, some official from the team brought us the bat Larry Walker had used to knock a two-run homer on the next pitch after our ill-fated foul ball. Walker had been kind enough to sign it and send it to Louise.

After examining Louise's arm, the doctor in charge suggested we go to a nearby hospital for an x-ray.

"No," Louise said, "I'd rather wait until we get home."

By that point, Louise was fully conscious and a little testy.

Louise and I were scheduled to be in New York the next day for the final round of the PGA Tournament, the last of golf's majors for the year (which Davis Love III would win). I was determined to see the PGA to go along with my visits to the U.S. Open and the Masters. In June, Ann and Jamie had accompanied me to the U.S. Open at the Congressional Country Club in suburban Washington, where we watched Ernie Els win his second Open championship.

Like any other sports fan, I had been thrilled to see Tiger Woods burn up the course at Augusta National, winning his first Masters by a record-setting 12 strokes. The most memorable moment of that Masters for me was watching Woods and Arnold Palmer visiting on the practice green, putting before they teed off for their first round. With the great Palmer nearing the end of his career, which has been mostly ceremonial on the regular tour for the last two decades, and Woods just beginning what many believe will be a dominating run, I felt like I was watching a historic encounter between golf's past and its future.

Since Louise and I were booked on an early morning flight for New York, I told Louise that we should go ahead to the hospital in Denver, since the Rockies officials were willing to help us out, rather than waiting until we got to New York where we wouldn't have an introduction at the hospital.

Louise glared at me. "New York, hell!" she exclaimed. "We're going to Birmingham!"

Hoping she would change her mind about the New York trip, I let the subject drop but insisted that we head on to the hospital in Denver. I wanted to make sure she had the proper medical treatment. The paramedics helped her into a wheelchair and rolled her down to the car.

About 15 minutes later, we pulled up to the Denver Medical Center, which was located in a bad area of town. The emergency room was like a war zone, filled with stabbing and gunshot victims. Given the presence of all those patients with life-threatening injuries, which placed us at the bottom of the priority list, it would take us four hours to confirm that Louise's arm was broken.

As we were sitting in an examination room waiting for the results of the x-ray, the hallway was full of angry voices. At one point, we heard some man running through the corridor shouting: "They shot my brother! I'm gonna waste 'em!" I quickly closed the door, hoping that he would not try to enter our room. We waited nervously and hoped that our ordeal would be over soon.

When the doctor finally returned with the x-ray, he confirmed that Louise's arm was broken. He advised us to put it in a cast, but Louise wanted to wait until we got home. So the doctor wrapped it and let us go.

It was well past midnight when we got back to our hotel, and naturally, Louise had trouble sleeping. After we returned to Birmingham the next day, she remained very uncomfortable until she went to an orthopedist, who put the arm in a cast.

Seeing that last batter certainly turned out to be an expensive ordeal, in more ways than one. I'm still paying for that trip. We were both surprised the day after we got home when a woman from the Rockies front office called to ask how Louise was doing, and to make a special point of letting us know that Larry Walker was concerned about her. Several days later, Louise received a letter from the Rockies offering her free VIP tickets to another Colorado game.

I doubt if we'll be heading back to Coors Field again, but to her credit, Louise remained a good sport and accompanied me to two other baseball games that season. However, she became very selective about her seat location.

In late September, for a Detroit Tigers-New York Yankees game at Tiger Stadium with John and Caroline Abele, we sat as far away from home plate as possible, in the left-field stands. In early October, we found ourselves with great seats behind first base at Camden Yards in Baltimore watching the Orioles host the Cleveland Indians in the second game of the American League Championship Series. But sitting so close to the action proved nerve-wracking for both of us so after the first inning, we traded seats with our friends Deak Nabers and John Kennedy, who were sitting a mile away in the upper deck, out of harm's way.

I have a feeling I'll be sitting in the cheap seats for the rest of my life. ■

CHAPTER EIGHT

"I Don't Want to Buy the Whole Gym, Just a Ticket!"

*E*verybody wants to know how I got my tickets. After spending a year on the road and attending all kinds of events, amateur and professional, blockbuster and obscure, I'm convinced that you can get a ticket to anything, as long as you're willing to pay the going rate. Sometimes the price was steep, but after making the decision to take the trip, I was determined to see the events on my list, regardless of the cost. Sometimes I was lucky enough to pay face value. Sometimes people gave me a ticket. Sometimes I had to pay an exorbitant price to a ticket broker.

Quite often, for the most important events, I erred on the side of caution by buying tickets from brokers before leaving for a particular event, which represented a certain amount of insurance. In many cases, I probably could have found a less expensive ticket from a scalper at the venue. But how foolish would you feel if you had flown thousands of miles to an event — at significant expense in airline, rental car and hotel charges — and then been unable to get a ticket? All because you had wanted to save a few dollars?

One of the toughest tickets in all sports, as most everyone knows, is The Masters golf tournament. There are people who have been on a waiting list for tickets to the prestigious event at the Augusta National for decades, and the club zealously guards any secondary sale of the tickets. Unless you know someone who has tickets, it's extremely difficult to get in. A long-time member of Augusta National who lives in Birmingham took an interest in my sports adventure and was kind enough to let me be his guest for the first round of the 1997 Masters.

On many occasions, I was fortunate to have friends who were eager to assist me in my quest and gave me free tickets. Bart Starr, the former Green Bay Packers Hall of Fame quarterback and coach, came through with a ticket for the San Francisco-Green Bay playoff game at Lambeau Field. Chuck Yob, a friend from Michigan, provided four free tickets to the Notre Dame-Michigan football game at Ann Arbor. Newt Reynolds, a friend and a New Orleans businessman, gave me box seats for the U.S. Open tennis tournament. Roy Rogers, the former Alabama star who's now playing in the NBA, left Louise and me two tickets for the Sacramento-Vancouver game. Bert and Teddy Salem, friends of ours from Tampa and two of the biggest North Carolina fans in the state of Florida, got me a ticket to the ACC basketball tournament as well as the North Carolina-North Carolina State game at the Dean Dome.

My buddy John McMahon has many friends in basketball and I'm glad. Not only did he come through with two very tough tickets to the North Carolina-Duke game at Cameron Indoor Stadium-which was one of the hardest sellouts of the year-he also got us into Fleet Center to see Rick Pitino's first game as the Celtics coach (against the Chicago Bulls and Michael Jordan), compliments of Pitino himself. In order to reciprocate, and to keep John from one-upping me, I gave the McMahons four tickets to one of the hardest tickets in Birmingham: ultimate fighting at Boutwell Auditorium!

In almost all cases, if you arrive early enough and are willing to pay enough, you can find a ticket outside a venue. But on several different occasions, there were no tickets to be had. The most obvious was The Masters. But some of the others might prove surprising, such as the National Finals Rodeo in Las Vegas, which was one of the hardest sellouts of the year. I had to pay several hundred dollars through a broker, and I was shocked. I thought they would be giving those away.

Some of the other tough tickets included the North Carolina-Duke basketball game, the fourth game of the Stanley Cup playoffs in Detroit, the Tyson-Holyfield heavyweight championship fight, the NBA's 50th anniversary All-Star Game, the Kentucky Derby, and the NCAA men's Final Four.

In many cases, parking was a problem. Sometimes, however, I learned that if you act like you belong, that's half the battle. On the day of the dedication game of the brand new Jack Kent Cooke Stadium in Washington, my friend Ben Dupuy picked me up at the airport and we drove hurriedly toward the stadium, with kickoff for the Washington Redskins-Arizona Cardinals game nearing. The next day, the media was filled with stories about the massive traffic and parking problems surrounding the new facility. But Ben and I had pulled right up to the stadium and conned our way into a lot very near our seats by yelling "Senator! Senator" at the police. They never asked for any identification. We just bluffed our way into a great parking place.

People often ask me how much I spent throughout the year on tickets. I'd rather not say. It would probably cost me another addition on the house if I let go of that state secret. People also want to know which tickets cost me the most. The most expensive was the fourth game of the Stanley Cup playoffs, in which Detroit defeated Philadelphia to clinch its first championship in 42 years. I probably paid more for that ticket than my daddy paid for his first house. He would probably turn over in his grave if he knew how much. The second most expensive was for the Holyfield-Tyson bout, which in retrospect was a big rip-off in several respects. You can be assured that neither Don King nor anyone in heavyweight boxing will ever get any more of my money.

At the end of June, I took time out from my tour around the Major League Baseball facilities to witness my first (and possibly last) heavyweight championship fight, Evander Holyfield vs. Mike Tyson. Jim and Guylene Jackson, two friends of ours from Birmingham, met Louise and me in Las Vegas the day before the fight. I had bought two tickets through a broker for Jim and myself. The girls had no interest in the fight and decided to soak up the atmosphere at nearby Caesar's Palace.

We arrived early so we could watch all the preliminaries, including female star Christy Martin, who knocked out Andrea DeShonge and managed to get beaten to a bloody pulp herself. I had never seen so many sports and Hollywood celebrities in one place. By the time the main event arrived, the whole arena at the MGM Grand was abuzz with anticipation. For the first two rounds, Holyfield handled Tyson quite easily. Midway through the third round, Tyson bit a chunk out of Holyfield's ear in one of the most bizarre sporting spectacles in recent memory. When this happened a second time, the referee stopped the fight, and Tyson started running around in the ring, swinging.

As Tyson was led out of the ring, a fight broke out in the stands and Jim and I became concerned about the possibility of a riot. We got out of there as quickly as we could, deciding to bypass the crowded lobby in favor of a side exit. Later, we found out that some crazed fan reported hearing a gunshot in the lobby, which led to a stampede in which 40 people were injured.

Of all the events I attended throughout the year, the Tyson-Holyfield fight was the only time I felt I had been taken. I wanted my money back, and worse, I felt as if I needed a shower.

It's unfortunate that a small minority of scam artists have given ticket brokering a bad name. During my travels, I discovered that most brokers and scalpers who sell tickets on the secondary market for a living are professional, hard-working, honest people. They take a certain amount of financial (and sometimes legal) risk in order to make a buck while providing a service that the sporting public demands.

On numerous occasions throughout the year, I dealt with Joni Carper at Golden Tickets, a Dallas company, and was amazed at their efficiency. The incredible number of events I attended made it crucial for me to retain some professional assistance, especially considering the need to obtain tickets at the last minute. Often, I would change plans on a daily basis depending upon the outcome of a playoff game, and Golden Tickets was of invaluable assistance in helping me attend all the events I wanted to see. Many times I would call with a specific need one day and Golden would have the tickets in my hands the next morning.

When I was in Cleveland for the Baseball All-Star Game, I went by the hotel where Golden Tickets was headquartered to disburse tickets to their customers. HBO Sports was in town preparing a report on ticket brokering, and they were in the suite interviewing Ram Silverman, executive vice president of Golden Tickets. When I went in to pick up my ticket, they interviewed me. I didn't think much about it until a couple of months later when several people called to tell me that they had seen me talking about the ticket brokerage business on HBO.

Although most of my experiences in procuring tickets were positive, I learned that when you don't deal with the professionals you're risking your money, legal problems and even bodily harm.

One case in point was the 50th anniversary NBA All-Star Game. I arrived early on the day before the big event in Cleveland in order to catch the rookie game. Tickets were hard to find for the main event, and I circled the arena looking for a good buy. Finally, I bought a ticket to the rookie game and the All-Star Game from a guy who looked pretty shady. It was not a very good ticket, so the next day, I walked around the arena trying to trade up, and I found a scalper who was willing to take my ticket and $50 and give me a better ticket in exchange.

When I gave him the ticket, he looked at me like I was trying to cheat him.

"What are you trying to do to me!" he said with an agitated tone.

"What do you mean?" I responded innocently.

"This is a counterfeit ticket!"

I had been scammed.

As it turned out, that guy was probably doing me a favor. Even though I suddenly found myself without a ticket to the game, if I had tried to use my phony ticket at the gate, I probably would have been arrested. I bought another ticket to the game and counted myself lucky.

In the days leading up to the Super Bowl between Green Bay and New England, tickets were fetching such high prices from the brokers that I decided to drive to New Orleans and take my chances. I felt comfortable in New Orleans, since I had been there so many times. I was certain I could find a ticket on the street.

After walking around Bourbon Street and Canal Street, I found ample tickets for sale in front of the Sheraton and Marriott hotels. Finally, I started closing a deal with a young man, and as we were exchanging money and ticket, one of his fellow scalpers rushed up and demanded to know what I was paying for the ticket. We told him, which led to a shouting match between the two scalpers. The three of us were clutching the ticket and the money, and none us wanted to let go.

I smelled another scam. I thought this might be some kind of routine they ran in order to cheat unsuspecting buyers out of tickets and money. They finally let go of the ticket and I let go of my money and I turned around and made a quick exit. Either they were scamming me or they were genuinely mad at each other, and I was afraid one of them might have a weapon.

In some cities, scalping tickets on the premises is legal. In some cities, it's not. I came face-to-face with the long arm of the law one night in Detroit.

After flying all the way to Detroit to see an early round Stanley Cup playoff game between the Red Wings and the Colorado Avalanche, I walked around Joe Lewis Arena for an hour looking for a ticket. But I didn't see a single ticket for sale. None. At any price. I began to think that I was going to miss my first event.

Finally, about five minutes before the face-off, I came upon a college student about 20 yards from the entrance. He had two tickets and was negotiating with a couple who needed only one, since they already had one. The young man insisted on selling them both tickets, so I told them I would take the other one off their hands. So we all exchanged money and tickets and an instant later, two undercover Detroit police officers stepped out of the shadows.

"You're under arrest," they told the stunned young man.

The couple and I immediately started walking to the arena. I just knew any second the police would be tapping me on the shoulder, but for some reason, they never bothered us. As we looked around from the door to the arena, they were escorting the guy off into the darkness.

The big ticket broker in the sky was looking out for me that night.

Toward the end of my year, I had planned to travel to College Station, Texas to attend the Texas-Texas A&M football game, one of the traditional rivalries that makes college football so special. However, Louise and Ann kept trying to persuade me to take them to Puerto Rico for Thanksgiving so they could revel in the warm weather. They even planned it so I could see the Puerto Rican Shoot-out basketball tournament. I was still paying for that broken arm, so we packed our bags for San Juan.

On the first day of a three-day tournament, Louisville was playing Hofstra, Illinois was facing Wichita State, Alabama was taking on Georgia Tech, and American University-Puerto Rico was hosting St. John's. Several years earlier, we had been to a similar tournament in the same small arena, equivalent to a high school gym, and I knew there would be no more than a few hundred fans on hand. Tickets would not be a problem.

I left Louise and Ann at the hotel and went by myself to the early game, walked up to the ticket window and tried to buy a ticket, but the lady told me that she could only sell the entire book of tickets for the whole tournament, which cost $180 each.

I thought to myself, "I don't want to buy the whole gym. Just a ticket."

Somewhat perturbed, I walked around to try to find a single-game ticket. There was only one ticket-taker, and I walked up to him and tried to ask him about getting a ticket. But he apparently only spoke Spanish and when I walked up to him, he just mumbled something in Spanish and motioned me into the gym.

Remembering how hard those old bleachers were, I had

brought a gym bag with two bed pillows borrowed from my hotel, as well as some newspapers I had planned to read between games. I walked in, found a seat and watched the final moments of Illinois' victory over Wichita State. Then I saw Louisville defeat Hofstra. There weren't more than 300 fans in the entire gym.

At halftime of the second game, I got hungry, so I left my bag at my seat and walked out of the gym, caught a cab to a nearby McDonald's and returned to the arena holding my sack of hamburgers. The same guy waved me in again.

When Alabama and Georgia Tech started warming up, I saw Louise being escorted by some strange man out onto the court, looking for me. "Edgar," she shouted when she finally spotted me in the stands, "this man let me in to get you . . . We need some tickets!"

"I'll meet you at the door," I yelled.

I had been sitting next to four other Alabama fans (perhaps the only other ones in attendance), Doug and Cindy Hollyhand and their two children. They are friends of David Hobbs, who was then the Alabama head coach. Doug had heard Louise's frantic plea.

"Come on," he said, "let's go over there and see if Skeeter Hobbs has some tickets . . ."

We walked around to the other side of the arena, and David Hobbs' wife kindly gave us one ticket. We then proceeded to the door, where the same Puerto Rican who had nonchalantly pointed me in twice, was standing with Louise. This time, for some reason, they were not going to let us in without buying three ticket books, which would have cost me $540.

I had already been allowed into the arena twice for free!

I was livid and I started shouting with this big guy from Illinois who turned out to be the sponsor of the tournament. About that time the Alabama players finished their warm-ups and headed back to the locker room, passing us on the way. They couldn't help hearing our shouting match. Louise, Ann and I were triple-teaming the American sponsor.

"You mean it's going to cost me $540 to see Alabama play one basketball game?" I demanded.

"That's right . . ."

I was already disappointed about having missed the Texas-Texas A&M football game for this relatively meaningless basketball tournament, and now I had come all this way and I wasn't going to be able to see Alabama play!?

"Well, I've been to every sporting event in the country this year and this is the most low-class, unprofessional, sorriest situation I've ever seen . . ."

He told us we would have to leave. "But I've got to go get my pillows!" I demanded.

Finally, after I returned with my bag, the guy decided to let us in. I think he had gotten tired of hearing an earful from Louise and Ann. We watched Alabama lose a close game to Georgia Tech. The next night, I was so infuriated by the whole ticket situation that I skipped 'Bama's second game, which the Tide lost to American University-Puerto Rico. Sometimes I still get angry thinking about that frustrating night in Puerto Rico.

There was one consolation to this whole situation. I watched the Texas-Texas A&M game on television the next day and it was played in a driving rainstorm. If I had made Louise suffer through that monsoon, I might never have heard the end of it.

At least the sun was shining in San Juan. ∎

CHAPTER NINE

First and Ten

During my youth in Wetumpka, we lived next door to Circuit Judge Oakley Melton and his wife, Dora, who taught all three of the Welden children in first grade. Their older son, Oakley, Jr., was a pretty good quarterback on the Wetumpka High School football team and went on to be president of the student body at the University of Alabama. During his senior year of high school, Oakley broke his arm playing in the final football game of the year against archrival Holtville on Thanksgiving Day. Shortly before that, the Wetumpka basketball coach had been drafted for service in World War II. Since Oakley couldn't play and the school needed a coach, the principal, O.M. Bratton, made the 16-year-old prodigy the youngest high school basketball coach in the country, attracting national attention. At the end of the season, after Oakley led the Indians to an impressive 18-7 record, Mr. Bratton, who later was my principal, rewarded Oakley with a crisp $50 bill, which was his compensation for the entire year.

Oakley's younger brother, Bimbo, was one of the best running backs ever produced in our area and earned a scholarship to play for the Crimson Tide in the early '50s. I remember when Bimbo broke his jaw returning the opening kickoff against Tennessee and he came home with it all wired up. To us, Bimbo was like a warrior home from battle and it was a big deal for all of us in the neighborhood to go over to his house and take turns feeding him through a straw. Later, the school developed a special helmet for Bimbo with an elaborate face mask, which led to his nickname as "the Man from Mars." That helmet is now enshrined in the Paul Bryant Museum on the University of Alabama campus.

Football has always been a powerful force in my life. When I was in the seventh grade, I skipped school one day and rode the bus to Auburn just to see football practice. Shug Jordan's program was one of the best in the country in those days — in 1957, the Tigers would capture the national championship, clinched by a 40-0 rout of Alabama — and I decided that seeing some of those players up close was more important than learning about history and science. When I got back, my teacher made me stay after school for several days, but it was worth it. About that time, I started playing organized football and eventually worked my way up to become the starting quarterback for Wetumpka High School. I probably would have had a real future if I had not been skinny, weak, and slow.

I was an Auburn fan during my formative years, but due to the influence of my older brother Charles, I decided to follow him to the University of Alabama. Over the next four years, I watched coach Paul "Bear" Bryant's Crimson Tide capture two national championships and lose a total of only four games. When I was a freshman in 1961, one of my fraternity brothers, senior Pat Trammell, quarterbacked Alabama's first national championship team of the Bryant era and was often described by the Bear as one of his finest players. I always liked what coach Bryant often said of the hard-nosed Trammell: "He can't run, he can't pass . . . All he can do is beat you!" For the last three years of my college career, our quarterback was a guy named Joe Namath. Perhaps you've heard of him.

After leading Alabama to an undefeated season and a national championship in 1964, Namath was hobbled with a severe knee injury heading into the Orange Bowl against Texas and was not expected to play. Steve Sloan, who had started several games in Namath's absence and would develop into an All-American quarterback in his own right, opened the Orange Bowl but was ineffective. In the second half, Namath came off the sidelines with his knee bandaged and led 'Bama from behind while playing one of the most inspiring games any of us had ever witnessed. In the final moments, Namath drove the Tide to within inches of a game-winning touchdown. On a fourth-and-goal keeper, every Alabama fan in the world believed Joe Willie scored, but the officials ruled that Texas, led by All-American linebacker Tommy Nobis, had denied him short of the goal line to preserve the Longhorns' 21-17 victory.

All these years later, the legend of that quarterback sneak remains a topic of debate for fans of both Alabama and Texas. On a recent visit to San Antonio as a member of the Republican site selection committee, I was delighted to meet long-time Texas head coach Darrell Royal and good-naturedly put him on the spot. Royal and Bryant were great friends and I enjoyed hearing stories about their days together in college football, but like the

Texas defensive line, he was not willing to grant me an inch on The Question. Royal assured me that Tommy Nobis had assured him that not only did Namath fail to score but furthermore, none of the Alabama offensive linemen penetrated the goal line.

Through the years, as I built a business and raised a family, my love of football never waned. My whole family enjoyed seeing the glory days of the Crimson Tide and incidentally, both my daughter Ann and my son Ed wound up following in their parents' footsteps by attending the University of Alabama. In 1990, when the World League of American Football was formed and Birmingham was awarded a franchise, I was fortunate to have the opportunity to become a minority partner in the Birmingham Fire. The franchise was majority owned by the Maloof family of New Mexico, who had previously owned the Houston Rockets of the NBA. Some of the other local minority owners included Larry Lemak, a prominent local orthopedic physician who also served as team doctor and later became the league's doctor, Richard Scrushy, chairman and CEO of HealthSouth, Thom Gossom, a television actor and former Auburn football player, and Steve Trimmier, a local attorney.

Although I was a very small limited partner, Louise and I enjoyed being involved with the team and my son Ed even worked in the football operations office for one season. We especially enjoyed the Fire's association with the franchises in London, Barcelona and Frankfurt, which gave us the opportunity to accompany the Fire to Europe and get to know the players, coaches and wives. Watching the Europeans react to the new experience of American football was interesting, and seeing the sport take its first tentative steps at Wimbley Stadium in London and Olympic Stadium in Barcelona, where we would return for the Summer Games in 1992, is something I will always remember. Out of our association with the team, we became friends with head coach Chan Gailey and his wife Laurie, assistant coach Pete Hurt (who later would become head coach at Samford University) as well as fellow limited partner Larry Lemak and his wife Georgine.

In my quest to see National Football League games in the midst of my 1997 sports vacation, my past association with Gailey and former Fire general manager Michael Huyghue paid off and helped make the experience more memorable. As this book was being written, Gailey was in his first year as head coach of the Dallas Cowboys, but during my year on the road, he was the offensive coordinator of the Pittsburgh Steelers and kindly arranged a sideline pass and a ticket in the stands for the Steelers-Baltimore Ravens game at Three Rivers Stadium. Huyghue, the vice president of football operations for the Jacksonville Jaguars, also got me a sideline pass and a ticket in the stands for the Jaguars-Steelers game at the Gator Bowl, where I tailgated with our friends Dick and Jackie Wilson, who live in Jacksonville. Jackie had played an important role in the early years of our business in Birmingham. Spending time with the Wilsons and getting to meet many of the avid Jaguars fans demonstrated to me how a city about the size of Birmingham can win a major sports franchise if there is enough community support.

During the fall, while also squeezing in post-season baseball and college football, my NFL experience took me to 15 games at

11 different stadiums, from frigid Lambeau Field in Green Bay to humid Irving Stadium, home of the Cowboys. I saw Buccaneers quarterback Trent Dilfer out duel future Hall of Famer Dan Marino to beat the Dolphins before a record crowd in Tampa. I saw Barry Sanders rush for 139 yards to lead Detroit to an upset over Green Bay. I saw Troy Aikman lead the Cowboys on a long touchdown drive in the final minutes to beat the Redskins, several days after being booed at a Mavericks basketball game. I saw Gus Frerotte hit Michael Westbrook for a 30-yard touchdown pass to lead the Redskins over the Arizona Cardinals in sudden death in the dedication game of Jack Kent Cooke Stadium in Washington.

Thanks to Chan Gailey and the sideline pass he graciously provided, my most memorable NFL experience of the year was my trip to Pittsburgh in November to see the Steelers host the Ravens.

Getting to watch the first half from the sidelines gave me a new perspective on the game. When I walked out onto the field, I felt self-conscious, as if everyone in Three Rivers Stadium was looking right at me. When you're watching from the stands or on television, you don't see the large group of support people all doing their jobs to make the system work, from the trainers furiously bandaging cuts to the assistant coaches wearing headphones and strategizing with their counterparts in the press box. You don't see how quick the action is and how difficult it is for the officials to concentrate on making the right call without getting run over. I came away from the experience with a great appreciation for the veteran NFL officials like Ronnie Baynes, an outstanding baseball coach at Mountain Brook High School who was an All-SEC end at Auburn in the 60s.

In the stands, you don't realize how isolated you are from the action, but when I was on the sidelines, I was amazed at how big and quick the players are, and I could see the intensity in their eyes. I could hear the crunching of the bodies, which made me think about the punishment the players must endure to play the game. I could listen to the banter at the line of scrimmage, especially between the wide receivers and the defensive backs. I could see the blood.

That afternoon, I had taken a side trip to the suburb of Harmarville to see a professional bowling tournament before returning to Pittsburgh and getting my game face on for the nationally televised Sunday night showdown. Someone on the airplane the day before had told me that the best way to experience the flavor of a Steelers game was to start off by having a few beers at one of the bars in the Market Square area along the riverfront, where hundreds of fans gather for pre-game warm-ups. Wanting to indulge myself as much as possible in the local color, I took the guy's advice. Several beers into my pre-game activities, I caught a ferry across the river to the stadium and mixed and mingled with early arrivals outside Three Rivers.

Standing around outside the stadium having a beer with several Steelers fans, our conversation eventually turned to the recently failed referendum which would have built a new football facility with tax money. The mostly blue-collar crowd near me had been opposed to public funding for a new stadium, even though all appeared to be big Steelers fans.

"I like to play checkers," one young man remarked, "but I don't ask the state to buy me a checkerboard. I have to buy my own checkerboard."

His buddy agreed. "Here I am working hard for my money and just getting by," he said. "Why should I pay for a place for these million-dollar players to work? Why can't they pay for it themselves?"

I was feeling pretty good by the time I got to the will call window to pick up my sideline pass. As I made my way to the field, one of the first people I encountered in the stadium was former Alabama All-American receiver Ozzie Newsome, the player personnel director for the Baltimore Ravens, who knows my friends Bruce Sokol and John Clements.

The Steelers, who entered the game with a 6-3 record and tied with Jacksonville for the lead in the AFC Central Division, capitalized on six Ravens turnovers in the first half to jump out to a 20-0 lead at halftime. Kordell Stewart, the Steelers quarterback, impressed me with his athletic ability. Given his background with an option offense at Colorado, I had never expected him to excel at the position in the NFL, but it looks as though he will have an outstanding pro career. After the game, I had the chance to visit with Stewart for a few minutes and I found him to be a very polite and classy young man.

After watching the first half on the sidelines, I ate a snack underneath the stadium with the sideline photographers and then made my way to my reserved seat at midfield between Chan's wife Laurie and their youngest son Andrew. Their older son Tate was in college at Auburn at the time. All around us sat family members of Steelers players and coaches, including the wives of assistants John Mitchell (who, along with Wilbur Jackson, had broken the color line at Alabama) and Mike Archer (the former LSU head coach), as well as front office personnel.

Even though the Steelers were comfortably ahead, I could feel a certain level of tension among all the wives, mothers and children. Even though I took my experience with the Birmingham Fire seriously and wanted the club to succeed, my life was never affected by whether the team won or lost. However, everyone sitting around me at Three Rivers Stadium that day had more than a rooting interest in the game. You could feel the intensity in the air. The anxiety was apparent among all those wives who knew that a loss could leave their husbands vulnerable to the wrath of an entire city, including being berated on the radio talk shows and in the newspapers. Knowing that every Sunday your husband's career hangs in the balance must be a very difficult way to live.

By the start of the fourth quarter, with the Steelers leading 30-0, I could sense the wives and mothers and sons and daughters around me relaxing, feeling assured of a Pittsburgh victory as they no longer focused so intently on every play and instead started truly enjoying themselves.

With the issue of the game decided, I wanted to know more about the coaching staff, so I asked Andrew to flip through the program and find the pages dealing with the assistants. At the time, Andrew was a senior in high school. He had been an outstanding end for his high school team, which had been eliminated from the playoffs the previous Friday night.

One section to our right and about five rows down, I noticed a commotion around three guys with bare painted chests. It was a quite chilly November evening and I thought they were pretty crazy to be standing out there without shirts on. They were making a lot of noise and everyone in our part of the stadium was looking at them. Except Andrew.

About that time, an attractive young brunette stood up in the middle of that group, raised her top over her head and shook her rear end and her bare breasts. Evidently, she had lost her bra. The three guys were hooting and hollering, which drew everyone's attention to the bare breasted young lady.

And I thought The Immaculate Reception was a sight to behold!

After exposing herself for a few moments, the young lady lowered her top and sat down. Andrew looked up from the job I had given him and seemed puzzled.

"What happened?" he asked.

I told him about the bare breasted lady who apparently had lost her bra, and he felt so left out.

"I missed it! Looking in this stupid program, I missed it! I can't believe I missed it!"

Then his mother, who was sitting to my right, laughingly said, "Andrew, you didn't need to see that, anyway!"

A few minutes later, after most everyone had refocused their attention toward the action on the field, she did it again. Determined to soak up as much of the Steelers mystique as possible, I had kept one eye focused in her direction, so luckily, I saw it happen for the second time. But Andrew missed it again and he was mad.

It was late in the fourth quarter and the Steelers had pulled out to a 37-0 lead when the television cameramen and many of the players on the field, having gotten caught up in the buzz of the brunette flasher, turned away from the game action and watched for her to do it a third time. By that point, you could hear random yells of "do it again" and "let's see what you got" echoing throughout several sections. Never had I seen the players on the sidelines distracted by some commotion in the stands, but most of the Steelers players on the sideline were looking at the girl instead of the line of scrimmage.

One of the distracted people on the sidelines was the teenager who was responsible for following Steelers head coach Bill Cowher to keep the cord from his headset from getting entangled. Several of the coaches' wives around me were laughing and pointing at the young man, who had his back to the field and was staring at the young woman. About that time, there was a long play and Cowher took off running toward the other end of the field, jerking the unsuspecting kid to the ground as all the wives burst out in laughter. Cowher may have been the only person on the sideline who hadn't sneaked a look at the topless girl.

After the game, I walked with Laurie and Andrew to the family waiting area adjacent to the coaches' offices and dressing room underneath the stadium. Chan introduced me to several of the coaches and other team officials, and I was especially delighted to meet Steelers owner Art Rooney, who seemed very interested in my year-long trip. Rooney has the reputation for running a first-class franchise and my visit reinforced this prevailing view.

My up-close view of the Pittsburgh Steelers organization was one of the highlights of my sporting adventure. It was impossible to walk through those halls and not feel the incredible history of all those Super Bowl champions and great players like Terry Bradshaw, Franco Harris and Mean Joe Green. The class of the organization was evident throughout the day, especially in the way so many of the players approached Andrew after the game and asked about his high school team, dispelling the prevailing image of the arrogant, self-absorbed professional athlete.

After we visited for awhile, Chan and his family dropped me off at my hotel in downtown Pittsburgh.

Several months later, I was elated when the Cowboys selected the former head coach of the Birmingham Fire, Troy State and Samford to replace Barry Switzer. I predict that Chan Gailey will have a long and successful career.

The previous January, I had launched my sports odyssey by traveling to see several of the pivotal games of the 1996 NFL playoffs, in which second-year expansion franchises Jacksonville and Carolina shocked everyone by advancing to the conference championship games and the Green Bay Packers returned to the Super Bowl for the first time in three decades.

It might surprise some people to find out that the Super Bowl was not a big priority for me. Most of the Super Bowls in recent years have been blowouts, and the event is filled with such hype that the game often takes on secondary importance to the party atmosphere surrounding the crowning of professional football's championship team. It's always such a big letdown. So while I was determined to go to Super Bowl XXXI in order to complete my big year, I headed off to New Orleans without being very excited about the trip.

Instead of flying to New Orleans, I drove from Birmingham to Tuscaloosa to see Alabama beat LSU in basketball on Saturday night, and then proceeded toward New Orleans with two of my young friends, David Browder and Kevin Rosamond. They had assisted me in some Republican political campaigns, and had never been to a Super Bowl. They were excited just to be going to New Orleans with the slim hope of finding two inexpensive tickets.

After spending the night in Hattiesburg, Mississippi, we arrived in New Orleans late Sunday morning and immediately headed for Bourbon Street. It took me several hours to find a ticket, and as I discussed earlier, that was one of the few times all year when I feared for my safety. The boys were just as excited about the possibilities offered by the French Quarter as the rare opportunity to see a Super Bowl, so rather than spending all their money on high-priced tickets, they decided to spend the afternoon partaking in the festivities of Bourbon Street.

To my surprise, I saw a good football game. Sitting in the lower section of one end zone, which is a good place to sit in the Superdome, I witnessed one of the most exciting Super Bowls in recent memory as Green Bay held off New England, 35-21, before a crowd of 78,344. It was great to see Green Bay finally return to the top after all those years, especially since I had been such a big Packers fan during the days when Vince Lombardi's team was led by former Alabama quarterback Bart Starr.

Anyone who loves football has to appreciate Packers quarterback Brett Favre. The former Southern Mississippi quarterback, who led the Golden Eagles to an upset of Alabama in Gene Stallings' head coaching debut in 1990, probably is not endowed with as much natural ability as Denver's John Elway or Miami's Dan Marino. But the guy plays with such intensity and heart. He has an incredible will to win. Of all the players I saw on my NFL tour, I would rank Favre as the most inspiring to watch. His gutsy determination reminds me of Pat Trammell, which for an Alabama man, is high praise indeed.

It can be difficult to analyze something so close to your heart as college football is to mine, but when I think about what makes the game special to me, two things stand out. One is the incredible tradition and pageantry. The history of winning at places like Alabama, Notre Dame and Michigan makes the game an experience filled with color and excitement. The other is the unpredictable nature of all those young men being asked to perform under such enormous pressure. Anything can happen, and often does. Sometimes a great player chokes and we're reminded he's just an amateur. Sometimes a player with relatively limited skills can amaze us and we cannot help feeling inspired.

In my college football tour across America, I saw 19 different games with a wide variety of experiences. The trip included blockbuster showdowns such as Notre Dame vs. Michigan at Ann Arbor; Tennessee vs. Florida at Gainesville; Kansas State vs. Nebraska at Lincoln; and Michigan vs. Penn State at State College. I also attended obscure match ups with no national significance, including Delaware vs. Villanova at Newark, Delaware; and Columbia vs. Holy Cross in New York City.

Scottie May, a political fund-raiser whom I had known previously, assisted me in getting to Ohio Stadium for the Ohio State-Wyoming game in Columbus honoring former Grambling coach Eddie Robinson, the winningest coach in NCAA history. Due to scheduling conflicts as I traversed the country watching other sporting events, some of the biggest games and most hallowed stadiums eluded me. I missed the Alabama-Auburn game, Texas-Texas A&M and UCLA-Southern Cal. Plus, I failed to see a game at Notre Dame Stadium, although I have attended games on the fabled South Bend campus in previous years.

One of the most enjoyable weekends of the football season was my trip to Lincoln, Nebraska, to see undefeated Nebraska host undefeated Kansas State. On Friday, I went over to an old gym on campus to watch the Nebraska women's volleyball team defeat Iowa State. I expected a few hundred people to show up, but was amazed to walk into a gym packed with about 4,000 die-hard fans for women's volleyball. On Saturday, I was able to experience Nebraska football with longtime Cornhusker fans Duane and Phyllis Acklie, who graciously hosted me and gave me a taste of what makes the team close to a religion in Nebraska. Like so many other families, the Acklies, including their grown children and grandchildren, plan their weekends around Nebraska football. It was the closest thing I have seen to matching the experience of Alabama football in intensity and emotion, with one major exception. Unlike the state of Alabama, where the rivalry between the Crimson Tide and the Auburn Tigers dominates so much, virtually every football fan in the state of Nebraska pulls for the Cornhuskers, which gives the program a rare distinction among major football powers and contributes greatly to their success. I sat with the Acklies in the president's box and watched Nebraska crush Kansas State, 52-26. The following January, I would be present in the Orange Bowl to see Nebraska overpower Tennessee, 42-17, to capture a share of the national championship in what would be Tom Osborne's final game as head coach.

Another memorable experience was my trip to Austin, Texas, where I toured the capitol as well as one of the meccas of college football, the University of Texas. Although the Longhorns were experiencing a rough season that would cost head coach John Mackovich his job, Texas looked impressive in beating Kansas, 45-31. Two of the Texas players put on an offensive show, senior quarterback James Brown and junior tailback Ricky Williams, who ran for 211 yards and was well on his way to becoming one of the leading rushers in college football history.

My host for the day was Gretchen Steen, who works in the scheduling office for Texas Governor George W. Bush. It was raining very hard that afternoon, so we waited out the monsoon for the entire first half at Scholz Garden, a rustic old tavern two blocks from the stadium. The famous watering hole claims to be the oldest tavern in the state of Texas and holds the oldest continuous business license in the state. As we waited out the rain, it was impossible not to sense the history of the place.

**August 17,
1997**
*Louise and Edgar
back home in
Birmingham with
two of Louise's
anniversary pre-
sents: a new arm
cast and her new
ball bat, gifts from
Larry Walker of
the Colorado
Rockies.*

**August 29,
1997**
New York City,
U.S. Open
Tennis
Tournament
*Edgar and
Ed at center
court.*

**August 31,
1997**
East Ruther-
ford,
New Jersey
NFL game:
Philadelphia
vs Giants
*Edgar at Giant
Stadium
at The Mead-
owlands.*

September 1, 1997
Providence,
Rhode Island
Ed and Danielle visiting with her family after a great Italian dinner. Left to right: Ed, Aunt Rosalie, Grandmother Rosalie, Danielle, Grandfather Gene and Uncle Tony.

September 4, 1997
Charlottesville, Virginia,
University of Virginia Campus
Auburn vs Virginia pre-game party
Edgar with Kelton Jones and Ben Dupuy.

September 12, 1997
Rochester, New Hampshire
Edgar with an unidentified winner of one of the Lumberjack contests at the 122nd Annual Rochester Fair.

September 20, 1997
University of Florida, Gainesville
Tailgating Party hosted by Hutch and Natalie Brock. Edgar with Gator Cheerleaders before the Florida vs Tennessee game.

October 2, 1997
Chicago, Illinois, WPA World
Nine-Ball Championships
Edgar with Jeanette Lee "The Black Widow" — World Ranking No.2 player.

September 27, 1997
Ann Arbor, Michigan
Notre Dame vs Michigan
Louise and Caroline Abele pregame. Louise wearing one of her anniversary gifts — the cast!

October 2, 1997
Chicago, Illinois, WPA World
Nine-Ball Championships
Edgar with Paul Gerni "The Ambassador of Pool" — 20 time winner of the World Trick Shot Championship.

October 2, 1997
Chicago, Illinois,
WPA World Nine-Ball
Championships
World Ranking Players celebrating following the competition — (left to right) Mary Guarino (USA), Edgar, Gerda Hofstatter (Austria), Helena Thornfeldt (Sweden) and Nikki Benish (USA).

October 9, 1997
Camden Yard, Baltimore, Maryland
Cleveland vs Baltimore Playoff Game.
Left to right: Morris Slingluff, Louise Red-
doch, Deak Nabers and John Kennedy.

October 17, 1997
Honolulu, Hawaii
Edgar with Mr. Sam Kamaka (left)
and Chris Kamaka (right) owners of
Kamaka Hawaii, Inc. in their
ukulele factory.

October 18, 1997
Kona, Hawaii
Edgar at the Finish Line of the
Ironman Triathlon

October 23, 1997
Cleveland, Ohio, Jacobs Field
Edgar at the 5th game of the World Series
— Cleveland Indians vs Florida Marlins.

October 31, 1997
Boston, Massachusetts, Celtics vs Chicago Bulls
First game with Rick Pitino as coach. Edgar with two fans — really dressed for the game.

October 31, 1997
Boston, Massachusetts
Post-game party hosted by Coach Rick Pitino
Left to right: John McMahon, Coach Pitino and Jim McWane. Coach Pitino is autographing a basketball for Pete and Derry Bunting to be auctioned at Highland Day School.

October 31, 1997
Boston, Massachusetts
Celtics vs Chicago Bulls
Betty McMahon pre-game wearing the Opening Night Big No. 1.

November 9, 1997
Harmerville, PA, The Brunswick Touring Players Championship
Edgar with bowler Walter Ray Williams, Jr., Bowler of the Year. Williams is also a six-time world horseshoe throwing champion.

November 9, 1997
Pittsburgh, Pennsylvania, Three Rivers Stadium
Edgar with Steeler quarterback Kordell Stewart and offensive coordinator Chan Gailey after the Steelers' big win over the Ravens.

November 9, 1997
Pittsburgh, Pennsylvania, Three Rivers Stadium
Edgar with some of the Pittsburgh assistant coaches' wives after the victory.

November 15, 1997
Austin, TX, University of Texas vs Kansas Football Game
Pre-game socializing at Scholz with Gretchen Steen and "the" bartender. Scholz is a couple of blocks from the stadium and is said to be the oldest bar in Texas.

November 21, 1997
Storrs, Connecticut
Women's pre-season NIT basketball game — University of Connecticut vs Nebraska
U of C President Dr. Phillip Austin (formerly Chancellor of the University of Alabama), Edgar and U of C Athletic Director Lewis Perkins.

November 22, 1997
Hartford, CT, World Tennis Doubles Championship
Ellis Ferreira with daughter, Camden and Dot.

December 6, 1997
East Rutherford, New Jersey
Edgar at the Army-Navy Game at The Meadowlands.

December 14, 1997
Las Vegas, Nevada
Edgar at the National Finals Rodeo

December 25, 1997
Montgomery, Alabama, Blue-Gray Game
Edgar with lifelong friend Joe McInnes and Joe's daughter Missy.

Back at the Ranch . . .
Ann and Edgar filing programs, ticket stubs and newspaper articles for an event. Each of these boxes holds one month's event files. (Photo courtesy of the *Mobile Press Register*)

December 1998
Edgar and his family at the completion of the book. Edgar and Louise; Ed holding Will, the latest addition to the Welden family; Danielle; Ann and Jamie.

Being a graduate of a Southeastern Conference university, I'm naturally biased in favor of SEC football. However, after seeing several games involving Big Ten teams, I came away with a great appreciation for that conference, especially how the alumni support the programs. In the SEC, partially because of our lack of professional sports tradition, the majority of our fans tend to be non alumni. But in the Big Ten, thanks to their much larger enrollments, most of the fans you meet actually attended the university they support.

I was surprised to find such incredible pageantry in the Big Ten, and such vociferous fans. Before embarking on my trip, I thought SEC football fans cared more about the sport and placed a greater emphasis on it than those from other areas of the country. It surprised me to learn that Big Ten fans are every bit as passionate and committed as those in the South.

The quality of play is roughly comparable, but I think the SEC ranks slightly higher because of the prevalence of skilled position players with great speed.

Several weeks before the college season started, I was in Washington for some meetings and found myself talking to many of the young people working on Capitol Hill. The subject of my sports trip invariably came up and after a while, I decided to host a party before the nationally televised Auburn-Virginia game on Thursday night, September 4, in Charlottesville. Ben Dupuy, who was an aide to Senator Jeff Sessions of Alabama, and Kelton Jones, who worked for Congressman Terry Everett of Alabama, volunteered to help with the arrangements. Ben, who had graduated from the University of Virginia, secured a prime party location: Jefferson Hall-Hotel C on the west range of The Lawn.

We invited fans from Washington and Alabama as well as students from Alabama who were in school at Virginia and other colleges in the area. Perhaps a couple hundred guests showed up for pre-game cocktails and hors d'oeuvres, including Dr. William Muse, president of Auburn University, and his wife Maureen. Also on hand were Tommy and Laura Susan Roberts, parents of John Allen Roberts, a senior on the Virginia team who had won the place kicking job, former Auburn player Billy Austin and his wife Ginger, and big Tigers fan Bill Ireland and his parents. After the party, we saw Auburn defeat Virginia, 28-14, behind the outstanding play of quarterback Dameyune Craig, who was one of the most exciting players I saw all year. I never understood quite what was going on, but all during the game, a large number of Virginia's students kept circling the stadium with drinks in their hands. I'm not sure they were that serious about the game.

What a contrast I found two days later. During Marshall's 35-25 victory over Army on the picturesque campus of the U.S. Military Academy overlooking the Hudson River in West Point, New York, everyone was focused on the matter at hand. There was no drinking, no partying, no dating. Football was the order of the day. If I ever have to go to war, I would rather be in a foxhole next to some of the Army cadets instead of some of those Virginia nomads.

Even though the overall caliber of athletic talent could not compare to what I was accustomed to witnessing in the SEC, I probably saw the best player in the country in Marshall wide receiver Randy Moss. He had touchdown passes of 90 and 79 yards, and even though the competition was not Michigan or Nebraska, he kept compiling the same kind of stats all year. Moss, who finished third in the Heisman voting behind Michigan defensive back and receiver Charles Woodson and Tennessee quarterback Peyton Manning, was so fast and so athletic that he made the defense look like they were running in slow motion.

It was a great thrill to visit West Point, which is steeped in history and tradition. I was given a tour of the Academy by Bill and Susie Harris, my long-time friends from Birmingham who now live in Washington. I joined them for the game. Their son, William, was a plebe at the Academy.

All my life I had heard about the magic of the Army-Navy game, so on the first Saturday in December, Louise and I traveled with our friends Charlie and Linda Stewart to New York City for the weekend. While the girls enjoyed the unrivaled Christmas atmosphere of New York City, Charlie and I traveled to the Meadowlands in New Jersey to see the classic showdown between the service academies. Looking back on the year, I must say that the Army-Navy game was my most unique college football experience, one that I recommend for anyone who enjoys the game. Army had won the previous five meetings by a total of 10 points, but Navy was a big favorite this time and wound up easily defeating the Cadets, 39-7. It was a sunny day but extremely cold as we watched the impressive sight of all those cadets from the Army and the midshipmen from the Navy line up on the field during pre-game ceremonies. I welled up with pride witnessing more than 8,000 of the country's best and brightest parade in front of us on that cold day, thinking about what they must endure in order to attend the academies and serve their country.

One of the highlights of the fall football season was attending the Notre Dame-Michigan game in Ann Arbor. This turned out to be a special weekend. Not only did I attend the Notre Dame-Michigan game, I was able to squeeze in a trip to my 28th and final baseball ballpark, Tiger Stadium in Detroit; attend the Sunday afternoon Green Bay-Detroit NFL game at Pontiac; and attend the Viking-Eagles game in Minneapolis on Sunday night — all in the same weekend! Louise flew up from Birmingham along with our friends John and Caroline Abele. Louise still had the cast on her arm and was a real trooper as we saw the Yankees beat the Tigers on Friday night.

One of the most interesting aspects of my season of college football was experiencing both extremes of the sport.

At one end of the spectrum, I watched eventual co-national champion Michigan defeat Notre Dame, 21-14, before a huge crowd of 106,508 at massive Michigan Stadium in Ann Arbor. The atmosphere of that afternoon is what makes big-time college football such a wonderful spectacle — Two legendary programs. National television. Boisterous fans. Electricity. Emotion. Big-time money. Big-time pressure. Gigantic bands playing two of the most famed fight songs in all of sports, over and over again. Some of the most talented players in the country competing against each other, with professional careers riding in the balance. The most celebrated athlete on the field that day, Michigan's two-way star Charles Woodson, would eventually win the Heisman Trophy and sign a multi-million dollar NFL contract based upon his accomplishments as a college player.

At the opposite end of the spectrum, I saw two Ivy League games in New York City on the same day three Saturdays later. First I ventured to the Columbia campus in upper Manhattan to see the Lions lose to Holy Cross, 45-16, before a crowd of about 3,300. Then I traveled to the Fordham campus in the Bronx, about 10 minutes away, to see the Rams lose to Dartmouth, 31-10, before a crowd of about 3,700. I walked up to the gate at both tiny stadiums and bought a ticket. There was no television, no blimp, no hype on the flip side of college football, without big money and big pressure.

The players at this level of college football do not receive athletic scholarships, so they are students first and foremost and they have no illusions about using their talents to make millions in the NFL. Yet what struck me about that afternoon was the intensity of the competitors on the field. To them it did not matter that football was an end into itself. It did not matter to them that they were playing in relative obscurity, before fewer fans than some high school teams attract in Alabama. Watching them in action, it was obvious how much they enjoy playing the game.

In one respect, the Columbia players have very little in common with their counterparts at Michigan. But the game is the common thread. They play the game because they love it, and that's what made both experiences so worthwhile. ■

CHAPTER TEN

"What Does the Miss America Pageant Have To Do With Sports?"

Generation Gap

In a world dominated by television, the major sports such as football, basketball and baseball tend to overshadow all the rest, rendering sports such as bowling, billiards, figure skating and the like to relative obscurity. But it takes just as much skill to bowl a perfect game as it does to hit a home run, and so as a sports fan in search of great athletic competition of all kinds, I was determined to travel the country and see as much variety as possible. It still amazes me that when I talk about my trip with friends or on the after-dinner circuit, more people seem to be interested in knowing about The Iditarod or the Ironman Triathalon than the World Series or the Super Bowl. They can turn on the television and see Brett Favre throw the long ball, and they understand the intricacies of football, but how many people know how you judge a lumberjack competition? To be honest, I saw a lumberjack competition and I still don't know how they judge it, but at least I can say I saw one. There's a mystery to many of these sporting events that take place beyond the big crowds, and I was determined to pull back the curtain for the sake of my own curiosity.

While TV certainly plays a very significant role in the pre-eminence of the major sports, it also has helped create a new generation of events that have greater worth as TV shows than for their in-person spectator interest. One of the most obvious is the X-Games, which is featured on the ESPN sports channel. In this Olympic-styled competition of and for the Generation X crowd, the variety of sport includes skysurfing, skateboarding, street luge, sportclimbing, bicycle stunting, wakeboarding, and bare-foot water skiing. Many of these unusual events have circuits of their own, in which the athletes travel around the country and in some cases around the world competing for prize money and perfecting their skills. Once in the summer, and once in the winter, the X-Games brings together several hundred of the very best competitors in sports most people my age have never seen.

Toward the end of June, on the heels of seeing the Stanley Cup Finals, the NBA Finals and the College World Series, I traveled to San Diego to watch the X-Games. Soon after arriving in one of the most beautiful cities in America and checking into The Bahia Hotel, I walked across the street to Mariner's Point Park, where much of the action was already underway. As I made my way into the park, I was struck by the very loud music pulsating through the air and the large crowd of young people who had shown up on a beautiful Sunday afternoon to watch several different events. I noticed they had a bicycle competition, which I could understand, so naturally, I gravitated to that area just as they were starting to practice.

When I was growing up in Wetumpka, I had a paper route for The Montgomery Advertiser, so I know all about riding a bicycle. My bicycle had a big basket on the front, and after I became really skilled at my job, I could, in one constant motion, pull a paper out of the basket, put a rubber-band around it, and send it flying in the general direction of the house in front of me. Of course, in those days, we were required by our customers to land the paper on the porch. Just throwing it in the yard wouldn't do. Having this athletic skill in my background, I thought I could relate to the bicycle competition at the X-Games.

Boy, was I wrong!

After a few minutes of watching the bicycle competitors, it was obvious to me that none of these guys had ever had a paper route. There wasn't a basket in sight. Instead of doing something useful, they were using their bodies and bikes to perform highly technical tricks that would have gotten me arrested in Wetumpka. Or at least sent to my room without supper. For example, one of the events had dirt jumpers vaulting from an 11-foot-high ramp, soaring into the air, twisting and spinning their bikes. Like gymnastics and figure-skating, the three different bike events are decided by judges who score the athletes based on how well they perform various skills.

The whole time I was watching this competition, I was struck by one thought: If they really wanted to have the athletes test their skills, they could see how many papers they could deliver before breakfast. I had a feeling that most of this crowd sleeps 'til noon.

The next day, I got to see sportclimbing, which is billed as one of the fastest-growing competitive sports in the world. This competition was held right there in the same park, at a man-made wall set up specifically for the X-Games. In this sport, men and women (competing separately) take turns trying to climb to the top of the mountain-like wall, with only suction cups to aid their climb. I also saw something called aggressive in-line skating, in which the competitors attempt to clear ramps, rails and bos jumps in an expression of skill and style.

The most popular event seemed to be skateboarding. In the street competition, the skaters must leap, jump and grind over an obstacle course while performing tricks such as "five-o grands" and "fifty-fifties." The precision and timing required to excel in this sport was amazing to watch.

After the first day, I went back to my hotel and called Louise. She asked me how I was enjoying the X-Games.

"Well," I told her, "not only am I the oldest person in attendance, I feel like I'm the only one without a tattoo or some sort of body-piercing!"

Whenever I went to an event, I always made a point of trying to meet new people and engage in conversation. But I found it difficult to do this at the X-Games. Most of the crowd was so young, and there was a noticeable generation gap. Finally, while I was observing one of the practice rounds for the bike jumping competition, I noticed two ladies about my age sitting off to the side. They seemed to be watching the competition very intently, and I thought they must know something about the sport, so I walked over and introduced myself and started talking to them. As it turned out, one of the ladies, Karen LeVan, was the mother of one of the bike competitors, Jimmy LeVan. The other lady was one of her friends from college days who lived in the San Diego area. The LeVans live in Nashville, Tennessee. Karen is involved in promotional marketing and songwriting. Twentysomething Jimmy is one of the top competitors on the circuit, although injuries kept him from finishing near the top at the X-Games. He competes full-time and had his own signature bike line with the Huffy bike company, which paid him to promote their products. Recently though, Jimmy has started his own bike company using his design, and initial reports are that his product is being well-received.

Karen's daughter, Susan, also rides on the bike tour and she eventually walked up and started talking with us as well. It seemed like everyone I saw had something pierced except for Susan, who is a very attractive young woman. So after talking with these nice folks for a while, I was just about to ask Susan what motivated young people to do all this piercing. Then she opened her mouth and I noticed a ring in her tongue. After that, I kept my mouth shut.

I really enjoyed getting to know the LeVans and seeing how this woman of my generation had adapted to the lifestyle of Generation X in order to be supportive of her children. I came to understand how these talented young athletes tour around the world and actually make a good living doing things most of the country knows little or nothing about. This lifestyle is foreign to me, but when you break it down to its most basic element, it really is no different than Louise and me supporting our children in whatever they want to do. The whole experience was enlightening, and gave me new insight into other people, places and events, which is exactly what my trip was all about.

Squeezed between college football, Major League Baseball and the other big-time sporting events, I managed to see a wide variety of lesser-publicized sports throughout the year, including the World Nine-Ball Billiards Championship in Chicago, the Ironman Triathalon in Hawaii, a lumberjack contest in New Hampshire, the National Finals Rodeo in Las Vegas, the championship of the Professional Bowlers Association in Pittsburgh, Binion's Horseshoe World Series of Poker in Las Vegas, and the U.S. Figure Skating Championships in Nashville.

Deal Me In

During the year leading up to the trip, an old fraternity brother from the University of Alabama, Banks Robertson, kept pushing me to add two off-beat sports to my agenda: The World Series of Poker and some big pool tournament. This all goes back to our college days, when Banks was more accomplished in these two areas than me. I had little experience with either one, but thanks to his prodding, I attended what turned out to be enjoyable events.

Each May, Binion's Casino in downtown Las Vegas hosts the World Series of Poker, so I added it to my schedule. After watching the Kentucky Derby on the first Saturday in May, I flew home to Birmingham that night and flew out the next day for Las Vegas. Going most anywhere out of Birmingham requires a change of planes in Atlanta. When I got to Atlanta, mechanical problems caused my Las Vegas flight to be canceled, so I was stranded in Atlanta overnight.

Luckily, there were two events going on in town that day. I went by Turner Field to watch a few innings of the Pirates playing the Braves and then proceeded over to the Omni to see the first round of the NBA Playoffs between the Hawks and the Detroit Pistons. Turns out my plane trouble was a lucky break. I got to see a very exciting game in which Christian Laettner and the Hawks eliminated Grant Hill and the Pistons from the playoffs. After spending the night in Atlanta, I got up early the next morning and caught a flight to Las Vegas.

Binion's is famous as the casino that has $1 million in cash encased behind glass in the lobby. Tourists often make pictures in front of this unusual sight. The casino controls the picture-taking and charges a few dollars for each snapshot. I'm sure they make much more off this steady stream of photographs than they would from the interest on the million dollars.

Since it was started in 1970, the poker tournament has also become a significant attraction for Binion's. It is the top poker event of the year, and gamblers from throughout the world participate, competing for millions in prize money. The tournament includes competitions in seven-card stud, Omaha high-low split, Texas hold 'em, and seven-card razz, among others.

Anyone can compete in one of the various preliminary games as long as they have the money. Buying into a table can cost anywhere from several hundred dollars to several thousand dollars. One satellite tournament, which may consist of a dozen different tables or more, can take several days to be played and wind up with a winner-takes-all pot of several hundred thousand dollars. The world championship is decided with a game of Texas hold 'em (no limit). There are typically about 300 entries in this game at $10,000 each, with the winner receiving $1 million.

I've never been much of a poker player, so as I walked around and watched several of the satellite tournaments, much of the strategy escaped me. I had intended to try to play in one of the preliminary games but I decided against it for fear that I would be exposed as a novice. Just like The Iditarod or the Boston Marathon, the World Series of Poker included professionals who make their living at the table and others who play just for fun.

The night I was there, I got to see the finals of one of the preliminary tournaments. Toward the back of the casino, there was a separate room with one big table surrounded by elevated bleacher seating. You could get close enough to the players to see their cards and hear the table banter. When I got there late in the afternoon, there were eight players still alive. Instead of sitting there for hours at a time, I would dart out periodically to check the pro basketball scores and watch the other poker satellite tournaments. Every time I came back in, someone else would be eliminated as the field dwindled. About five hours later, I was sitting in the stands when some guy from Columbus, Ohio, won $231,000.

One of the most interesting aspects of watching the poker tournament was observing the appearance and actions of the competitors. There was incredible diversity among the players, ranging from men in expensive suits and excessive jewelry to men in sweat suits and others in blue jeans and cowboy boots. I saw a scruffy looking guy with a ponytail and several Asian businessmen with hundred-dollar haircuts.

One table could offer an incredible range of personalities or poker faces. With thousands of dollars riding on every card, it was interesting to see how some players handled the pressure. Some wore icy expressions and rarely uttered a word. Others seemed at ease and friendly.

Unlike most of the events I attended throughout the year, I didn't make any new friends at the World Series of Poker. All of the people around me were very serious students of the game and had no interest in idle conversation. I kept asking people very rudimentary questions about the various games and they kept staring back at me like I was a nut. It was yet another occasion when I felt like people wondered: Who is he? Where is he from? And why is he here?

After I left Las Vegas and I flew to Salt Lake City to catch the Utah Jazz and the Los Angeles Lakers NBA playoff game, I was back in my element. I didn't have to ask stupid questions. The Jazz won an exciting victory in spite of former Alabama star Robert Horry leading the Lakers with a record-setting seven-of-seven from three-point range. I was surprised when a Jazz fan sitting next to me kept yelling for Horry to shoot every time he touched the ball. After Horry made three straight, I asked the guy why he kept yelling. The guy had no reason. I told him to quit yelling because I knew from experience when Horry gets hot, he can hit all night.

I then caught a flight to Houston to catch another NBA playoff game between the Rockets and the Seattle Supersonics. It was a battle of the stars: Charles Barkley for Houston and Shawn Kemp for the Sonics. The Sonics beat the Rockets 106-101.

It was great to be back watching a game I actually understood.

Strike!

As I crisscrossed the country during the fall watching college and professional football, I was able to schedule a side trip to the suburbs of Pittsburgh to experience another kind of championship. After going to picturesque State College to see Michigan beat Penn State in college football, I drove to Pittsburgh, where the Steelers would be playing the Baltimore Ravens on Sunday night. I had purposely scheduled this trip so I could spend Sunday afternoon watching the biggest men's bowling event of the year in Harmarville, Pennsylvania, before that night's NFL game.

The Brunswick Touring Players Championship, the last stop on the Professional Bowlers Association tour, featured only the top touring pros. The day I was there, qualifying was still underway and I got to see all of the bowlers. It was a very casual atmosphere. There were only a few hundred people in the stands and the bowlers were very accessible and glad to pose for pictures and talk with the fans.

Between games, I spent some time talking with Walter Ray Williams, Jr., a four-time PBA "Player of the Year" and the all-time leading money winner on the tour. Walter, who seemed very interested in my trip, is also a six-time world horseshoe throwing champion. I was disappointed to learn that I had missed the World Horseshoe Championships.

When I was a teenager in Wetumpka, it was a big deal to get our parents to drive us all the way to Montgomery to go to the new bowling alley. It was air conditioned when very few places had that modern convenience. I remember in those days, before automatic pin setters, our fun often came at the expense of the human pin setters. They would sit back behind the lanes, in a crouched position, waiting for us to roll and we would do our best to hit them.

My most recent experience with bowling happened several years ago when we were at the beach with another couple, Charlie and Linda Stewart. It had rained at the beach for several days and we were starting to get cabin fever, so we headed for the bowling alley. Louise beat me! That day served only to confirm my long-standing belief that bowlers are not athletes!

But seriously, after watching the best professional bowlers, you cannot help being impressed by their skill in knowing how to place the ball at a specific location. The bowlers themselves are accustomed to the "they're not really athletes" argument, but it is instructive to realize that within the course of one 42-game tournament, players will lift more than five tons, carrying the ball for a total of two miles while projecting it more than 700 times at an average speed of 17 miles per hour at a target 60 feet away.

The Woodchoppers Ball

The lumberjack contest may be one of the oldest forms of sport in America. Many of these events have their roots in state fairs in certain areas of the country, particularly in the northwest and the northeast, where logging has always been a significant part of the economy. After working for several months to find a contest that we could fit into my schedule, we found an event at the 122nd annual Rochester Fair in Rochester, New Hampshire. So I flew into Boston on Friday, September 12, rented a car and drove 75 miles north to attend Woodsmen Day at the Rochester Fair.

In many ways, this local fair was just like the ones we had back home when I was young. There were livestock contests, baking competitions, clown dunking, quilting, and many other events which have continued over more than a century. In addition to the lumberjack contest I had come to see, they also had a harness race. I had always heard about harness racing and was glad I saw it for the first time at this historic fair.

The main event for the day was the lumberjack competition, which had drawn men and women from throughout New Hampshire and surrounding states to compete in a contest of sawing and cutting. The men and women competed in separate divisions. For the most part these were not professionals; they tended to be outdoorsmen and women who had developed their particular skills as a hobby.

Several hundred people crowded around a fenced-in area where the lumberjacks competed in several different events, including log rolling, two-man cross-cut, one-man cross-cut, modified chain saw, and axe throwing. I thought all of the competitions took a tremendous amount of skill and strength.

The most amazing thing I saw was something called the standing block chop, where they stood on the top of this log and chopped away with full force of the axe, within inches of their feet. One wrong move and they could have chopped their foot off. Luckily, these people were all very skilled.

The Ambassador & The Widow

Two years before I started this trip, Louise and I bought a pool table for our house at Lake Martin. Our good friends and lakeside neighbors, Fred and Mimi Renneker, bought one at the same time and we started developing our meager skills. Both of us bought nice tables which far exceeded our abilities. I had never played much pool growing up, but always wanted to learn more about the game, so when I decided to make this sports trip, I decided I should include a pool tournament, especially considering the encouragement of my friend Banks Robertson.

Instead of attending some ordinary pool tournament, I was able to schedule a trip to Chicago for the most prestigious pool tournament in the world: the World Nine-Ball Championships, hosted by the Billiard Congress of America. The tournament was held in a large ballroom at the Sheraton in Arlington Heights, with both men's and women's divisions. Several hundred people watched from temporary bleachers erected around eight different tables. As I learned more about the sport, I discovered that various promoters are pushing to make pool an Olympic sport, with the hopes that it will be accorded this special status sometime early in the next century.

In watching these professionals play nine-ball, it was impossible for me to deny the finesse and touch required to excel at the sport. Nine-ball, which is the game that was featured in the 1996 movie, "The Color of Money," is considered one of the most difficult forms of pocket billiards. At the start of each game, balls 1 through 9 are racked in a diamond configuration. The 1-ball is the head ball, and the 9-ball is located at the center of the rack. On all shots, the lowest numbered ball must be contacted first. The balls are thus played in rotation, with all pocketed balls counting as long as the stroke is legal. The player who makes the 9-ball at any stage of the game, as long as the lowest-numbered ball is contacted first, wins.

Between matches, many of the competitors congregated around the adjoining bar, and it was easy to engage them in conversation. I had my picture made with Helena Thornhardt of Sweden, the world's fifth-ranked player, and three other top players who seemed flattered that I would come such a long way to see the tournament.

That day I met the director of the tournament, Peg Ledman. Several months later, she would come to Birmingham to discuss the possibility of the Mountain Brook Inn hosting a future billiards tournament.

In contrast to the days of my youth when the image of the local pool hall in Wetumpka was of a dingy, poorly-lit dungeon where unemployed slackers whiled away the hours gambling, my first experience with professional billiards was quite an eye-opener. The whole event resonated with class. All of the men and women competitors were dressed in formal wear.

One of the nicest, classiest people I met was Paul Gerni, known as "The Ambassador of Pool" and pool's "Grand Master of Trick Shots." Paul, who has won the World Trick Shot Championship an unbeleievable 20 times, is truly an ambassador for the sport of pool. His special project has been to help cue sports gain Olympic recognition.

Probably the biggest draw of the tournament for both men and women was the world's No. 2-ranked player, Jeanette Lee, better known as "the Black Widow." This slender, sensuous, dark-skinned Asian woman is always dressed elegantly and in all black. She's an outstanding player. The combination of looks and talent makes her the most watched player on the circuit.

Several months after the tournament, I woke up in the middle of the night and was unable to get back to sleep. So I turned on the television in our bedroom and started flipping through the channels. Finally, I came across a pool tournament on ESPN and I punched Louise, who was sound asleep.

"Wake up, honey!" I said excitedly. "There's my friend, the Black Widow!"

Louise was not amused by my obvious infatuation. "Edgar," she said with an exasperated tone. "Shut up, turn the TV off and quit dreaming."

Ride 'Em, Cowboy!

When I think back on the rodeos of my youth, when we would travel from Wetumpka to the Coliseum in Montgomery to see the Southeastern Championship Rodeo, the things I remember most are the clowns, the grand entry of the horses and their colorful riders, and the wild bucking broncos. In February, right before I left for The Iditarod, the Alabama Jubilee Championship Rodeo came to Birmingham and I was in town on a Sunday, so I decided to go to my first rodeo in 45 years. The young sons of two of my friends had expressed an interest in going with me to one of my sporting events, so I thought it would be interesting to take them to a rodeo. Jerry Duncan and I took his seven-year-old son Luke and his two friends, Peyton Falkenburg and Dennis Elder, to the rodeo at the Birmingham-Jefferson Civic Center.

All these years later, I found myself appreciating different things about the rodeo, especially the incredible athletic skills of the riders. The competitors who ride the broncos and rope the calves must be very fit, agile, and mentally alert. Also, much like the mushers and the dogs at The Iditarod, the rodeo riders and the animals have a symbiotic relationship that cannot be overstated.

The following December, as my tour was coming to an end, my wife and children wanted me to take them to Las Vegas for a fun-filled long weekend. I decided to plan the trip so I could attend the National Finals Rodeo at the Thomas Mack Arena. The event was a hard sellout of 17,000 for ten consecutive nights, and to my surprise, this would be one of the toughest tickets of the year.

I loved the action-packed, fast-moving aspects of this world-class event. I was lucky to be there on the final afternoon, when Dan Mortensen won the overall championship, unseating two-time defending champion Joe Devere. The categories included bare-back riding, steer wrestling, team roping, saddle bronco riding, calf roping, bull riding, and barrel racing. Victor Deck of Summerdale, Alabama, had a good showing in the steer wrestling, finishing 15th and in the money.

The rest of the family skipped the rodeo to go shopping and do other things, so I went by myself. It was Louise's birthday, and

I still don't understand why she wouldn't accept her birthday present — a ticket to the rodeo.

Zero Percent Body Fat

During the third week in October, I sacrificed a football weekend so I could fly to Hawaii, to attend the legendary Ironman Triathalon and also tour the state capitol. Soon after I arrived in Honolulu, I checked into the Hilton Hawaiian Village, and then took a cab to the capitol for a tour. After finishing my tour, I started looking around outside for a cab and I saw a man sitting in his pickup truck with his child and asked him where I could find a taxi. He was waiting to pick up his wife, who worked in the governor's office. He kindly offered to call me a taxi from his cellular phone.

While I was waiting for the cab, we started talking and he told me that he owned a ukulele manufacturing business. One thing led to another and he offered to give me a personal tour of his factory, so I made plans to show up there the next morning.

The next day, Friday, October 17, I got up early and toured the University of Hawaii and Aloha Stadium (where they play the NFL Pro Bowl as well as the college Aloha Bowl) and then took a taxi to the ukulele shop. Chris Kamaka, the guy I had met the day before, was very nice and started taking me on a tour of his small shop, considered the top manufacturer of hand-made ukuleles in Hawaii. You could see the incredible pride they took in their work, and it was evident that little had changed since Chris' grandfather started the business in 1916.

I met Chris' father, who asked me where I was from.

"Alabama," I said proudly.

"Well, where's your banjo," he asked jokingly.

I ended up buying two ukuleles as presents for my son Ed and my son-in-law Jamie. I'm sure that was exactly what both guys wanted for Christmas. Later that day, when I went to the airport to fly off to the big island, I stopped to check my bags and the lady at the counter saw that I was carrying two ukulele cases. She asked me where I got them and I told her.

"Oh, that's Sam's place," she said, referring to Chris' father.

It turned out that Chris' brother was a pilot for Aloha Airlines and everyone on the island knew about Kamaka Hawaii, Inc. and the Kamaka family.

Such a small world. I felt like I was back in Wetumpka.

After a 40-minute flight to Kailua Kona on the big island of Hawaii, I took a cab to the Royal Kona Hotel, which is located about a mile from the site of the next day's Ironman Triathalon. I walked around and spent some time figuring out a plan for the next day. There are several shops and restaurants that face the water, and as I walked around, I came upon Dave Scott, one of the most famous triathletes in the world, who was signing autographs. I bought a hat and had him sign it for DeeDee and Bruce Sokol, who are long-time competitive runners. On my way to Hawaii, I had read a book written by Bruce about DeeDee's courageous battle against cancer, so they were on my mind.

The next morning, I got up early and headed over to Kailua Pier, where I stood on the steps of a retail store on Alii, which gave me a good view of the start of the Triathalon. After walking the mile from my hotel, I was already worn-out. Then I started to think about what an incredible event this was, how these 1,477 athletes had to be in amazing shape to swim 2.4 miles, bike 112 miles, and then run 26.2 miles. All in the same day! As I looked out on the start of the swim and saw all those hard, lean bodies, I figured I must have accounted for half the body fat on the entire island.

Just qualifying for the Ironman takes a high level of previous accomplishment. You can't just enter. You must qualify by virtue of placing high in various regional triathalons. Competitors converge on Hawaii every year from around the globe, so the field from top to bottom represents some of the world's greatest athletes.

When they lined up to start the swim, someone blew an airhorn, which the swimmers mistakenly took for the starting signal. In reality, the race is supposed to start with the firing of a cannon. So for the first time in the history of the Ironman, they had a false start and were forced to call the swimmers back to the starting line. The public address system started calling for them to come back, but they couldn't hear. So several of the official boats moved in to block the swimmers and force them back for a second start.

After the official start the swimmers were off again. After swimming around a marker and back, the athletes pulled themselves out of the water and onto the pier, where their bicycles were waiting. The line of 1,477 bicycles on that pier is impressive, and whenever a particular athlete comes out of the water, an aide is waiting with his bike. They don't towel off or spend any time resting. They just put their shoes on, jump on those bikes and go.

After racing for 112 miles around the island, where, on this particular day, the temperatures of the pavement reached 120 degrees and the stiff wind was more of a factor than usual, the athletes then jumped off their bikes and ran the last 26.2 miles back to the original starting area along the ocean front. While they were biking and running, I went back to my hotel and watched Alabama lose to Tennessee and Auburn lose to Florida in football. Then, that afternoon at 3 o'clock, I walked back to the start/finish line, where thousands of people had gathered to see the climax of the Ironman. As the athletes crossed the finish line, some of them were staggering. Others looked like they could run another marathon.

First place went to German competitor Thomas Hellriegel, who finished in 8 hours, 33 minutes and 1 second. Amazingly, he swam his leg in 53 minutes and 8 seconds; biked the second leg in 4 hours, 47 minutes and 57 seconds; and then ran the marathon in 2 hours, 51 minutes and 56 seconds. The first woman finisher was Canadian competitor Heather Fuhr, who completed the course in 9 hours, 31 minutes and 43 seconds. Both male and female winners were awarded $35,000.

Close behind Fuhr were two other women who collapsed of exhaustion about 10 yards from the finish line. But both women showed their determination by crawling the rest of the way, which leads me to perhaps the most surprising fact of the whole event: Of the 1,477 competitors who started the race, 1,368 finished.

The tales of endurance so common to the Ironman go way beyond statistics.

Several times a week, I eat breakfast at The Anchorage

restaurant in Homewood, where Linda Baker serves up grits, eggs and toast with a smile. Many mornings I see fellow diner and realtor Johnny Montgomery, the No. 1-ranked triathlete in the Southeast in the 50-55 age group. Johnny expected to be a serious contender in his category at the Ironman in 1997, but he was involved in a serious bicycle accident a few months before the Ironman. Yet he still had the determination to compete in the event and actually finished.

For hours after the first athletes finish the Ironman, thousands of people gathered around the various establishments along the oceanfront, creating a party atmosphere. Every so often, another runner stumbled across the finish line, having accomplished one of the most incredible feats in all of sports.

Local Boy Does Good

John Zimmerman had been dreaming of this moment his entire life. Zimmerman, who grew up in the Birmingham suburb of Homewood, was 23 years old and just hitting his stride as an athlete when he took to the ice to compete in the U.S. Figure Skating Championships at Nashville Arena on Friday, Valentine's Day, February 14, 1997. He and his partner, Stephanie Stiegler, needed to finish in the top three to qualify for the world championships.

I had gotten to know John a couple years earlier through mutual friends, and had been part of a small group of local people who encouraged him to further his dream. His mother and father had worked hard to promote his quest to become a world-class figure skater, almost dedicating their lives to his dream. But training is expensive. John worked odd jobs around town to supplement his income while training full-time at the rink, so it was especially gratifying for me to see such a nice young man work his way up and have the chance to be considered one of the best in the world.

By the time Louise and I arrived in Nashville on Thursday night, John and Stephanie had already qualified for the finals. The next night, the pressure was on. The team of Jenni Meno-Todd Sand were heavy favorites in the pairs competition, but the event marked a changing of the guard as Kyoko Ina-Jason Dungjen captured first place. Meno-Sand finished second. Zimmerman-Stiegler skated next-to-last and turned in a terrific performance, placing them neck-and-neck with Lyons-Wells, who skated last. John and Stephanie had finished fourth behind Lyons-Wells the previous year. But in competition separated only by a razor's edge, Zimmerman-Stiegler finished third and advanced to the world championships.

As I watched the competition, I remembered the few times I've tried to ice skate, most of them ending with me on my rear end. In contrast, it was amazing to see the athletic skill those skaters possessed, not merely in skating with great precision and dancing with incredible grace, but in performing various maneuvers and in the case of the men, holding their partners aloft without missing a beat.

Knowing someone who has worked his whole life to attain a goal and then being there to see it happen made the night special. I felt vested in his success. I also felt so proud for John's parents, Norma and John Zimmerman, whose hard work and sacrifice had paid off. It was a wonderful moment for their whole family. As this book was going to press, John had become partners with Kyoko Ina, who had finished first with her partner at the 1997 championships, so now the sky is the limit as they go in search of Olympic gold.

LLWS

After attending the Huggy Bear Tennis Tournament on Long Island, New York in mid-August, I planned to drive to Williamsport, Pennsylvania, for the Little League World Series. But a snafu with my driver's license almost left me stranded in the middle of nowhere.

I didn't want to fight the traffic of New York City and suburban New Jersey on a Friday afternoon, so I hired a driver to take me into Pennsylvania, where I planned to rent a car and drive the rest of the way. Well, the plan worked beautifully until the driver dropped me off at a rental car counter in Mount Arlington, Pennsylvania. It wasn't exactly a bustling metropolis; in fact, the rental counter was located above a service station.

Although I didn't realize it until I pulled out my wallet, I had left my driver's license at the hotel in Southampton, where they had required me to show it when I checked in and forgot to give it back to me. As anyone who travels knows all too well, it's difficult to rent a car or fly without a driver's license. In fact, it's supposed to be impossible. At first, the rental car people were not the least bit accommodating. They said there was no way they could rent me a car without a driver's license, and I had no other options. This was a very small community in the middle of the Pennsylvania countryside, and there was no taxi-cab, no bus, no airport. If I couldn't rent a car, I might never get out of there. It was like an episode of The Twilight Zone.

Luckily, I have one of the most efficient secretaries in the world. Somewhere in her files back at my office in Birmingham, she found a photostat of my driver's license. After more than an hour of trying to convince the lady at the rental counter that I wasn't some maniac, she finally agreed to rent me a car with that photostat. Karen also called ahead to one of the airlines to make sure they would let me get on the plane two days later with the copy of my license. So I was able to rent the car and drive on to Williamsport.

On Friday night, I watched the International All-Stars defeat the American All-Stars in extra innings. The next morning, I got up and drove across town to tour the original Little League field, where they played the game from 1947-58. Above the stadium hung the flags from the states of all the winning teams through those early years, including Alabama's. On the center field wall hung a sign commemorating the 1953 victory by Southside of Birmingham. Through the years, I've gotten to know Ed Donahue, who played on that team and later starred as an athlete at Ramsey High School and became a successful high school coach in Alabama and in Georgia.

Surprisingly, on a day when the big game across town would attract 35,000 fans and a national television audience on ABC Sports, perhaps 50 people were milling around the historic original stadium. Before that day, I wasn't aware of the rift that had occurred between Carl E. Stotz, the founder of the game, and his board of directors over the future of the game in the 1950s. While in Williamsport I learned how Stotz had parted ways with the board over what he saw as the encroaching commercialization of the event. They eventually kicked him out and moved the game across town. The controversy went to court and he was banned from interfering with the event.

In contrast to the old stadium, which was decorated mainly with souvenir photos and game balls, the Peter J. McGovern Little League World Series Museum offered all the modern amenities: video displays, hands-on exhibits, a 60-foot running track, archives, etc. After soaking up a little history, I walked to the outfield, where thousands of people bring their lawn chairs or sit on the grass to watch the game. I had decided the night before not to worry about trying to find a seat in the stands at Howard J. Lemade Stadium.

I thought sitting on the grass would be more fun, and when I got there, there were some nice people who had an extra lawn chair and invited me to join them. It was a real comfortable atmosphere. One of the funny things to me was watching how the kids brought pieces of cardboard and used them to slide down the bank. The couple's teenage son, Steven Fichthorn, struck up a conversation with me, and before I left, I asked him to get a copy of the next day's local newspaper for me, as a souvenir from the game. He sent it to me as I asked, and ever since, we've been pen pals. I've tried to repay his kindness by sending him souvenirs from my travels, especially t-shirts and baseball caps.

Since so many kids across the country play little league baseball, the Little League World Series is a special event unparalleled in American sports. At an age when the kids are still learning about competition and the joy of the game, the spectacle strikes to the heart of all of our memories of youth. Heading into the bottom of the sixth and final inning, California led 4-1 and was three outs from the championship. But Mexico pitcher Gabriel Alvaren hit a three-run homer to lead a miraculous rally, which tied the game and eventually led to a 5-4 Mexico victory. The American crowd was stunned, but it was an exciting finish.

As I drove out of Williamsport that afternoon heading for New York City, I was struck by the incredible beauty of the hills of Pennsylvania. It was one of the prettiest drives of the entire year, thanks in no small measure to the quick thinking of my able secretary.

Alaska Point Guard

When I told Louise that I was heading off to the Miss America pageant during the second week in September, she naturally wanted to know why.

"What does the Miss America pageant have to do with sports?" she demanded.

I was prepared for this inquisition. To be totally honest, I've always wanted to go to the Miss America pageant in Atlantic City, New Jersey, which like all red-blooded American boys, I watched on television. In junior high and high school, we would take our dates to somebody's house and handicap the contests, choosing our favorites and making fun of the rest. The pageant always fascinated me, especially the talent competition. The girls from our region of the country were always — by far — the prettiest!

When I decided to take my sports trip, I was determined to go to the Miss America pageant, no matter how creative I had to be in coming up with an excuse. One day I read in the newspaper that a guard on the women's basketball team for the University of Alaska-Anchorage, Michelle Marie Titus, would be representing her state in the contest. Boom! I had a connection! Of course, later on, Louise found out that 1997 was the first year the pageant would be allowing two-piece bathing suits. I tried to convince Louise there was no connection and that I had not heard of this change, but I don't think she believed me.

After checking into the Bally's Park Place Hotel, I made my way down the crowded boardwalk to the Atlantic City Convention Center. The room was abuzz with excitement. Many people were talking about the controversial rules change allowing the contestants to wear two-piece bathing suits. Only 13 out of 51 contestants decided to wear two-piece suits, but evidently, they were a big hit with the judges. Five of the 10 semi-finalists had worn two-piece suits, in addition to three out of the final five and the winner. There were also new hosts (soap opera stars John Callahan and Eva LaRue Callahan) and several changes to the format of the contest. I sat next to the man who ran the preliminary pageants in both California and Nevada and he briefed me on the background of the girls and the preliminaries.

When the judges reduced the field to five finalists, I found myself pulling for Miss Mississippi, Myra Barginear, who had attended the University of South Alabama in Mobile. But she finished as second runner up, behind first runner up Miss North Carolina and the winner, Miss Illinois, Katherine Shindle, a senior at Northwestern University.

The next morning, I caught an early morning flight on a tiny turbo prop from Atlantic City to Philadelphia and found myself sitting next to a pretty young lady who was holding a yellow hula hoop. I wasn't quite sure why she was holding a yellow hula hoop. Frankly, I was concerned that it might violate some FAA regulation to be holding a yellow hula hoop in her arms. I wanted to call the flight attendant over and ask her to make this pretty young lady stow her yellow hula hoop, so the yellow hula hoop would not violate FAA regulations and perhaps strangle me in the event of a crash. I wondered what my mother (much less my wife) would think if my mangled body were found entwined with a young girl and a yellow hula hoop. I could see the obituary in the next Wetumpka Herald: "Birmingham businessman dies in hula hoop-related crash . . ." (This would have been the biggest story in Wetumpka since the night Tommy Head fell in the well . . .)

But eventually, I struck up a conversation with her and it turned out that she was Miss Florida, Christi Neuman, who had been a semi-finalist the night before. The hula hoop was her talent.

Sitting across the aisle from us was famed defense attorney Gerry Spence from Jackson Hole, Wyoming, who had been one of the judges for the pageant. Believe it or not, he was wearing a buckskin coat with fringe and cowboy boots. I wondered if he wore that outfit to bed. Spence started talking to Miss Florida and indicated that he had been supportive of her. He told her he thought she should have been a finalist.

Miss Florida expressed concern that she had not been able to perform at the top of her game because she was second in line. "I didn't have time to limber up," she said.

Then Spence said, "Oh, I gave you a 10 anyway. Of course I gave everybody 10s. I thought everybody was good. I gave everybody a 10. They probably won't invite me back, but I thought everybody was good . . . "

And Louise told me this wasn't a sport!

When we arrived in Philadelphia less than half an hour after we departed Atlantic City, Gerry Spence and his wife boarded a plane for Wyoming, Miss Florida and her hula hoop boarded a plane for Jacksonville, and I boarded a plane for Washington to catch that afternoon's Washington Redskins-Arizona Cardinals football game, the first contest in the brand new Jack Kent Cooke Stadium.

I was heading back to the "real" sports world — or had I ever really left? ∎

CHAPTER ELEVEN

Love and Love

Tennis has always been my favorite sport. I came by my love for the game naturally. My parents, Vic and Dot, built a clay tennis court in their backyard at some point in the 1940s, which was highly unusual for a small town like Wetumpka in those days. As my brother Charles and I started gravitating to sports in the 1950s, at the same time that our parents became busier with work and raising us, we took over the tennis court area to make our own basketball court, complete with two goals. After the city built a community center one block away, with two asphalt tennis courts, we spent a large amount of our formative years learning to love the game.

In those days, tennis was basically a country club sport, and there was no country club in Wetumpka. It was tough for us to get up a game. I'll bet there were less than ten kids my age who knew how to play in the entire county. But the ones who played really loved the game, and when I was a junior in high school, four or five of us got together and started a tennis team at Wetumpka High School. We didn't have a coach. We didn't have uniforms. We didn't even have a schedule. But you hear all those stories from the good old days when people talk about not having this or that and having to make their own fun. Well, we made our own fun by starting this team and basically challenging some of the high schools who had teams to play us.

Very few of the small-town schools in the state of Alabama had tennis teams in those days. One of the rare ones was Benjamin Russell High School in Alexander City, where we played on Roberta Allison's home court. Roberta, who was about our age, was part of the Russell family, which founded the world-famous Russell Corporation, and in high school was one of the top tennis players in America. Later, when we were at the University of Alabama, she was the first female athlete in the history of the school. They didn't have women's teams in those days, so she played on the men's tennis team and was one of the outstanding players of her era.

I think our entire schedule consisted of our home and away "series" with Alexander City. Needless to say, Alex City was our biggest tennis rival.

Every year the state tournament was held in Sylacauga and the hearty souls on the Wetumpka team naturally thought we could whip anybody. Well, not really. But we just wanted to find an excuse to get out of school for a day. The school hadn't appropriated any money for tennis, so we had to approach one of the local civic clubs to pay our entry fee and our travel expenses to Sylacauga, 40 miles away! When we all lost on the first day, the most disappointing thing of all was that we couldn't return the next days and miss another day of school.

At the Birmingham Country Club, we have a tennis group

called "The Turkeys." The name is more of a comment on the quality of play than anything else. This group is not to be confused with "The Grand Masters," another bunch of infamous tennis players at the club. Our "Turkey Tennis" group does not consist of the best players at the club, but we all enjoy the game. Fred Renneker is our czar. He makes all the rules and comes up with the schedule. In order to play on Sunday afternoon, you must call the czar's office during the week and sign up.

Every so often, someone will complain, and Fred will be ready with his standard reply: "You want to be the czar? Well, here, do all the work and you can have it . . . " Czar Nicholas of Russia, he isn't. He keeps the job because no one else will do it, nor could anyone else do it as well.

Each May, "The Turkeys", which consists of about two dozen members, holds a tournament and an auction. In the days leading up to the tournament, a "secret committee" of our group meets in the men's room at the Greyhound bus station in downtown Birmingham to assemble the pairings. Then they present the pairings at the Friday night dinner, where we must also suffer through raunchy skits. Then we bid on each others' teams. The next day, we play the tournament. Through the years, I've finished anywhere from first to last.

My mother has always been a big sports fan, particularly of tennis and college basketball. When I first started talking about taking a year off to attend sporting events, she offered plenty of encouragement. Unlike some members of my family, she didn't think I was nuts. Of course, she got a couple of trips out of the deal, including one to the NCAA Final Four in Indianapolis and another to the World Doubles Championships in Hartford, Connecticut. Most years, the whole family goes to the SEC basketball tournament, which typically coincides with mother's birthday. Louise and I, along with our children, my mother, my sister Vicki, my brother Charles and his wife Mary, and even Charles and Mary's 2-month-old son McNicholas and 2-year-old daughter Kathleen have attended this family event. We're often amazed at mother's stamina. During my sports year, Louise and I often found ourselves dead tired and just wanting to go to sleep when mother wanted to go out and attend more events.

Even though I have played tennis my whole life, it took an Alabama football game to get me to the U.S. Open for the first time. In 1986, the Crimson Tide played (and beat) Ohio State in the Kickoff Classic at the Meadowlands in East Rutherford, New Jersey. Louise and I decided to take a side trip to the U.S. Open, which is played in the Flushing Meadow section of the borough of Queens. That experience really hooked me. Since then, we've only missed one or two U.S. Opens, so naturally, the event was one of the first I penciled-in for 1997.

When you watch tennis on television, most of the coverage is limited to the big singles matches at center court, but since I started going to the U.S. Open, I've learned to enjoy watching the doubles matches. I'm a doubles player myself, and the game is totally different from singles. It takes teamwork to be a good doubles player, and plus, you can be a good doubles player without being especially talented or fast if you know how to play smart. To me, doubles is a faster-paced game and the points come quicker, which makes it a better spectator sport. At the U.S. Open, most of the crowds gather to watch the big singles matches, so when you go off to the side courts to watch doubles, you can get closer to the players and get more involved in the action.

In recent years, my interest in watching doubles has grown thanks to the success of two of my friends on the circuit, Brent Haygarth and Ellis Ferreira. Our relationship goes back to an Association of Tennis Professionals satellite tournament several years ago in Birmingham called the Eddleman Tennis Classic. The day before the real tournament started, I played in the pro-am with Brent, who is from South Africa. At the time, Louise, Ann, and our good friend Fred Renneker and his daughter Charlotte were planning a trip to South Africa for the following month. So I invited Brent to dinner to pick his brain about what to antici-pate in his native country, and we became friends with Brent and his wife, Monica, who was accompanying him on the tennis tour.

At the pro-am event, Brent and I competed against another South African, Ellis Ferreira. Even before we took the court, I was familiar with Ellis, who had been an All-American at Alabama. Some time before, Warren Ruttenburg, who also played on the Alabama tennis team and is a good friend of my son Ed, had told me that he thought Ellis would be one of the best doubles players in the world. And he was right. Both Ellis and Warren have rocketed to the top since they graduated from college. Warren's family founded Just for Feet, the Birmingham-based athletic shoe chain, which has experienced amazing growth since Warren joined the company.

Two decades after moving from Forest Hills to Flushing Mead-ow, the U.S. Open christened the new Arthur Ashe Stadium at the Flushing Meadow site several days before I arrived in the middle of the 1997 tournament. The highlight of the event for me was watching Martina Hingis defeat Venus Williams in the women's singles final. It was clear to me that these two outstanding young players will be facing each other with championships on the line for years to come.

In addition to the U.S. Open, I squeezed four other tennis trips into my year. In March, I attended the Lipton's Championship in Miami, but was disappointed to have missed both Ellis and Brent, who were knocked out of the tournament before I got there. In July, I traveled to Newport, Rhode Island, to see the Hall of Fame Championship tennis tournament, home of the International Lawn Tennis Hall of Fame and Museum. The Newport Casino Club hosted the forerunner of the U.S. Open from 1881-1915, before it moved to New York. Through some business contacts, my nephew Chuck Welden was able to wrangle an invitation for us to play the historic grass courts. We played two members, Alex Cushing and his wife Nancy Wendt. Alex and Nancy have a home in Newport, Rhode Island, and Squaw Valley, California, where Alex was instrumental in luring the Winter Olympics to Squaw Valley in 1960.

In August, I traveled to Long Island, New York, to attend the Huggy Bear Tennis Tournament, a pro-am event contested every year before the U.S. Open. Five wealthy brothers host the tournament, rotating it among their own private courts. Big prize money attracts many of the top doubles players, including my friends Brent Haygarth and Ellis Ferreira, who arranged for me to be invited to the players' dinner, where I met many of the star players, including tennis great Ken Rosewall and golf legend Jack

Nicklaus, two celebrities who played in the tournament.

In September, I traveled to Washington, D.C., to see the U.S. defeat Australia in Davis Cup play. Kate Hollis, who works in Senator Jeff Sessions' office on Capitol Hill, accompanied me to the match, which featured exciting victories by Pete Sampras over Mark Philippoussis and Michael Chang over Patrick Rafner.

On his day off from the U.S. Open, Ellis Ferreira joined us for Sunday brunch, where we celebrated the birth of his first child, daughter Camden, who had been born several weeks earlier. His wife Ashley was at home in Atlanta with the baby. As the rest of the family went off to shop, Ellis and I headed for Giants Stadium to see the New York Giants defeat the Philadelphia Eagles in football, 31-17. Even though he grew up in South Africa, Ellis has developed into a huge football fan. Several years before, Ellis had been our guest at the Alabama-Auburn football game in Birmingham. During the same trip, we pulled a little trick on some of my friends at the Birmingham Country Club.

Billy Walker and Joe Jolly were the best over-55 doubles team in the state of Alabama. It had long been my goal to beat them, but my partners and I were never good enough to give them much competition. Well, when Ellis came down for the Alabama-Auburn game, I called Billy and told him my cousin, Bubba Welden, from my hometown of Wetumpka, was coming up for the Iron Bowl and we wanted to play some tennis. Even though he knew we probably wouldn't give them much competition, Billy kindly agreed to play us that weekend.

They didn't know I had a 25-year-old ringer.

For most of the first set, Ellis, a.k.a. Bubba, held back and just played average, like a tennis version of Paul Newman in "The Hustler." Eventually, he started hitting some amazing shots and it was clear that I was in the process of defeating Walker and Jolly for the first time! Around the end of the first set, I pulled my two opponents aside and let them in on my little secret . . . that they were competing against one of the best doubles players in the world! Naturally, we won.

After the match, as we were relaxing in the clubhouse, Joe was still in denial: "During warm-ups, he looked pretty good. But I still thought I could take him!"

Unfortunately, in November 1997, I was forced to choose between my love of tennis and my love of Alabama football. I decided to skip the Alabama-Auburn game, one of the most intense rivalries in college football and the most important sporting event every year in my state, to travel with Louise and Dot to Hartford, Connecticut, to see the World Doubles Championships. As I mentioned earlier, I've always enjoyed going to tournaments and watching the doubles matches, and to see the best players in the world would be a real treat. Adding even more incentive was the presence of my friend Ellis and his partner Patrick Galbraith, who entered the tournament ranked third in the world.

As Ellis's personal guests for the weekend, we were met at the airport by tournament officials and escorted to the Goodwin Hotel, the official hotel of the tournament, which was located right across the street from the Hartford Civic Center, site of the matches. My mother got a real kick out of the whole trip. We got to meet several of the best players in the world, including No. 1-ranked Mark Woodforde at breakfast in the hotel restaurant.

He's one half of the famed "Woodies" team, along with Todd Woodbridge, who are closing in on the record for grand slam doubles championships. Dot told him that she often watched him play on television. She also kept staring at his naturally curly red hair, and finally told him, "It's a shame to waste that beautiful hair on you, instead of a girl."

Ellis arranged tickets for us in the VIP section, immediately behind the court. We were able to meet and mingle with many of the celebrities, including K.C. Jones, the long-time Boston Celtics star and coach, and Fred Stolle, the former tennis champion who's now a tennis commentator for ESPN. It wasn't the first time I had met Fred. A couple of years before, he had ventured to Birmingham to be our guest at a special tennis weekend at the club. Fred stayed at the Mountain Brook Inn, and on the way to the club, he and I stopped at our house for drinks. While Louise and I were socializing with this legendary tennis figure, our son Ed telephoned from Florida to announce his engagement to Danielle, so Fred Stolle will always be linked with that special moment in our lives.

Later that same evening, we hosted a function at the club for Fred and, in addition to our tennis-playing members, we invited several of the golfers. The Birmingham Country Club has always had the reputation for being more of a golf club than a tennis club, so Fred, who is a very gregarious Aussie, had some fun with several of our golfers, standing around telling stories at the cocktail party.

"I would take up golf," he finally said to them, "except I'm still sexually active!"

However, my sister-in-law Mary, who is one of the top amateur golfers in the state, and my brother Charles, who is 59, certainly contradict that statement, since they have two children under the age of three.

Even with their own personal cheering section in Hartford, Ellis and Patrick lost their first match to a team that eventually advanced to the finals. They won their second match and were eliminated in their third match. A former No. 1 player, Rick Leach, and his partner, Jonathan Stark, won the tournament, defeating the team of Leander Peas-Mahesh Bhupathi, 6-3, 6-4, 7-6(3).

One morning going down to breakfast at the hotel, my mother lost her footing on a marble step and injured her knee. Later that day, while we were at the tournament, the knee was still bothering Dot, so Ellis took her down to the locker room to have the trainer look at it and the trainer said she would be fine. Truth is, mother was so excited to be in the locker room around all those great players, she probably forgot all about the pain.

Most people see professional tennis as a glamorous haven of millionaires, but below the top echelon players like Andre Agassi and Pete Sampras, the tour consists mainly of people struggling to make a decent living. It was instructive for me to watch those matches with Ellis's wife, Ashley, a University of Georgia graduate, and their daughter Camden. Ashley tended to get very nervous during the matches; sometimes, when the action got especially nerve-wracking, she would pick up the baby and walk away from the courts.

I'm a very intense sports fan, and I was sweating every point for my friend, but I'm sure I cannot fully comprehend the anxiety of knowing that one shot or one umpire's call can make a tremendous difference in your ranking, and therefore, your income. Over the last several years, I've watched Ellis claw his way from relative obscurity to become one of the top doubles players in the world, and I have gained a real appreciation for the incredible dedication required to determine the hair-splitting difference between No. 1 and No. 50 in the world. Ellis is one of the fortunate ones; he makes a good living. But sitting there with his wife and seeing the intensity in her eyes, knowing that thousands of dollars of their income could be decided on a few points, it was easy to see that these players were not just going through the motions. Every point means something.

On the same trip, I had planned to travel to the University of Connecticut in Storrs, about 40 miles from Hartford, to visit my friend Phil Austin, the president of the school, as well as to see Connecticut host Nebraska in the finals of the Women's Pre-Season NIT basketball tournament. On Friday morning, we went down to breakfast in Hartford and were getting ready to go to Storrs for the day. Sitting next to us were several ladies dressed in warm-up suits, and I thought they were involved somehow in the tennis tournament, so we struck up a conversation. But it turned out that they were referees for that day's semifinal matches in the NCAA women's field hockey championship tournament, which would be held that afternoon on the University of Connecticut campus.

After looking at the morning's paper, I had already decided to attend that afternoon's field hockey games, even though I didn't know a puck from a stick. And I didn't have a ticket. So when I told them I was going, they seemed shocked that some guy with a Southern accent who had never seen a field hockey game in his life was going to spend his afternoon trying to learn something about the game.Louise and Dot decided to do some sightseeing and shopping in Hartford, so I dropped them off at a mall and headed to Storrs in my rental car. I got there in time to see the late morning game between Princeton and North Carolina. I just walked up to the gate and bought a ticket. Never having been exposed to the sport, I discovered that it is basically a combination of soccer and hockey. They play on a grass field roughly the size of a soccer field but instead of a soccer ball, they use a smaller ball and knock it back and forth with a stick. It's hard to get excited about a game when you don't know any of the rules, but it was the semi-finals of the national championship, so I enjoyed the experience. To them, it was as important as it would have been to me if Alabama had been playing in the Final Four of the men's basketball tournament.

Between games, I left to tour the campus. When I got back to the field, the game between Virginia and Old Dominion had already started. I was standing next to a fence watching the action near two ladies who turned out to be coaches for teams who were not involved in the tournament. I started asking them questions about the sport, and they finally said, "Where are you from, anyway?"

About that time, I heard the public address announcer say, "Would Edgar Welden please report to the press box! Edgar Welden!"

So I asked those two ladies where the press box was.

"Why?"

"Well, they're calling me to the press box . . . "

"Why do they want you in the press box?" one them asked.

"Well, I guess they want me to tell them something about this game . . . "

I walked off with a grin as they looked confused.

After making my way to the press box, I was met by a uniformed university police officer who informed me that President Austin had called from New York, where he had meetings that day, to say that he would be late getting home and that the officer would escort me to the president's mansion. We were supposed to have drinks that evening. But I wanted to stay and watch the end of game, so I sat down in the press box next to all the NCAA officials. All of a sudden, I had the best seat in the house and all those people had no idea that I didn't belong there. So I started asking the people seated next to me all kinds of questions about the game, simple stuff like, "Is that a hard ball or a soft ball?" and "How much of a curve is there on the base of that stick?" They quickly got annoyed at my stupid questions and wondered what business such a novice had being in the press box.

Finally, one of them asked, in a flippant tone, "Who do you coach for, anyway?"

"Oh, I'm not a college coach. I'm here to select the next Olympic team!"

They didn't know what to say. I guess some of them thought I was serious. By their expressions I guess they thought the American Olympic team must be in real trouble.

A lady at the other end of the press box overheard the conversation and finally got up to take a closer look at me. "Hey, aren't you that guy from breakfast this morning?"

After Old Dominion defeated Virginia, I met the uniformed officer at the gate and he escorted me to the president's mansion. But neither Phil nor his wife, Susan, were home yet. The Austins also have a home in Hartford and Susan had been delayed with the kids and was expected to arrive a short time later.

I had known Dr. Austin since his days as the chancellor of the University of Alabama System. He had moved to Alabama after serving as president of Colorado State University. After spending several years as the chancellor of the Alabama system which is tied so closely to big-time college football, and fighting for funding with several other major universities, Dr. Austin had been attracted by the University of Connecticut because the state legislature had recently pledged an additional $1 billion over the next ten years for capital improvements and other special projects. Even though he had moved to a school where football had never been much of a factor, Phil walked right into a major controversy over the future of the football program, which many of the alumni wanted to upgrade to Division 1-A, and the building of a proposed stadium. How ironic that he had left Alabama, where everything is driven by football, and had gone to a non-football school where he found himself embroiled in a major political battle, not over academics, but over football.

As I sat in his living room by myself, having made myself at home drinking wine and munching on cheese and crackers while reflecting on his predicament, I heard a knock at the door. I got up and answered it, just like it was my own house. I opened the front door to find this cab driver with a confused look on his face.

"Is this the president's mansion?"

"Yes."

"Well, I've got two women out here in the cab for you."

I looked out and saw it was Louise and Dot. I ushered them in like I owned the place.

Not long afterward, Phil arrived from New York and Susan and the boys (Patrick and P.J.) arrived from Hartford. We spent about an hour visiting and reminiscing about our mutual friends, including Mac Portera. Phil and I got on the phone and tried to call Mac and congratulate him on his recent appointment as president of Mississippi State University, but we couldn't reach him.

After a while, it was time for us to go to the basketball game. We all sat in the president's seats at mid-court and got to meet various university officials, including the athletic director. Gampel Arena was packed. Women's basketball is huge at Connecticut and the fans take the game very seriously. The most valuable player in the tournament, Nykesha Sales, would later be involved in a national controversy. She was on her way to breaking the all-time UConn scoring record when she sustained an injury late in her senior season. With Sales only one point shy of the record, her coaches arranged for her to be allowed to make an uncontested layup to set the record and then be pulled out of the game. This led to protests among basketball purists who believe the record was meaningless if it could be broken in such a way.

Connecticut would end up winning the game, 71-61, but we

had to leave at the half so we could get back to Hartford to see Ellis Ferreira and Patrick Galbraith play a late match. They lost, so the next day, we gathered at my hotel room to watch the Alabama-Auburn game. After Alabama fumbled in the final moments to set up a game-winning Auburn field goal, I was glad I had chosen to spend the weekend in Connecticut.

The next morning, as we were waiting in the lobby for our host committee to take us and the Ferreiras to the airport, we visited for a few minutes with Alex O'Brien, who had lost a tight match in the previous day's semi-finals of the World Doubles Championships. Alex was supposed to be catching a flight to Sweden that morning to play in the Davis Cup. It would have been the first time he had represented his country in this prestigious international competition, but he was obviously crushed, because during the tournament, he had developed a stress fracture in his foot and was instead heading home to Texas for rehab. I had met Alex during his visit to the Eddleman Tennis Classic several years before when he was staying at the Mountain Brook Inn. I felt bad for his loss. I could only imagine how disappointed I would have been in his circumstances.

When we were flying back to Birmingham that day, I couldn't help reflecting on the trip to Connecticut and, in a larger sense, the underlying reasons for my year on the road. As much as a celebration of games, I wanted the year to be a time for me to seize the day and do all those things I had been talking about and dreaming about for so long. You never know how many years you have in this life. Among other things, the trip allowed me an opportunity to spend some quality time with my mother, and the memories of that week will live with me forever. ■

CHAPTER TWELVE

Catching the Dream

*A*round *the Welden household in Wetumpka, Christmas was a bittersweet time of year. Although all of us kids got out of school the week before the big day, my brother Charles and I worked at my daddy's grocery store and didn't get much of a vacation. It was a tradition in those days for the small-town grocery stores to set up a Christmas stand on the sidewalk in front of the store, and instead of playing touch football or riding bicycles, we spent our vacation days selling oranges, apples, tangerines, sparklers, Christmas trees and an assortment of candies and nuts. It was usually very cold, especially after the sun went down, and we wanted to be anywhere else but out in the weather sacking fruit and parching peanuts. We tried to sell as much as we could, because many of the items that didn't move wound up in our stockings on Christmas morning.*

Like all good boys and girls, we anticipated Christmas Day, anxiously awaiting what we would find under the tree. But for us, the day meant even more than getting presents. It meant a day off, because we didn't have to work on Christmas Day. Many years my stocking would have tickets to the Blue-Gray Game at

Cramton Bowl in Montgomery, which was a major sporting event to me at that point in my life. In those days, television showed very few sporting events, and only a small number of college teams played in bowl games. This meant that more big-name players were available for the all-star game, featuring selected players from the north against selected players from the south. In today's terms, it probably would have been the equivalent of the Major League All-Star Game in importance to me.

After launching my year-long sporting adventure on the day after Christmas in 1996, it seemed natural to culminate it exactly one year later by attending the 1997 Blue-Gray Game on Christmas Day. My mother had asked me what I wanted for Christmas, and I told her I wanted two tickets to the Blue-Gray Game. She kindly granted my wish and I started making preparations to see Montgomery's biggest annual sporting event for the first time in more than three decades.

Unfortunately, the game starts at 11 a.m. on Christmas morning, which helps it attract a huge national television audience but also places it in conflict with many family holiday activities. You should have heard all the excuses I was given by people I asked to accompany me to the game. I must have asked 20 different people to go with me, but found no takers. Most people had legitimate family reasons why they couldn't go, but it became quite obvious that some others were willing to make up anything not to go with me. My wife later told me I should write a book called, "Why I Can't Go to the Blue-Gray Game With Edgar . . . "

My friend Warren Lightfoot stumbled around for a few moments before coming up with a good excuse: "Oh, I usually spend Christmas Day afternoon raking leaves!"

The morning of the game, when I was no more than six blocks from Cramton Bowl, I finally called my friend Mary Gantt to see if she or her husband Butch would go. "Thanks," Butch said, "I'd like to go, but I had planned to wash my truck!"

I still wonder why I asked my mother for two tickets.

On Christmas morning, even though we had no children at home, I awoke early in my own bed in Birmingham and started the final day of my adventure. On the way to Montgomery's Cramton Bowl, I would stop to see my mother and my Aunt Jean, who had lived next door to us while we were growing up and who had been like a second mother to me. There's been a standing family joke for 50 years that Aunt Jean taught me to close the bathroom door and to always put the toilet seat down after using the bathroom.

Since I could not convince even Louise to go to the Blue-Gray Game with me, I found myself alone at the wheel, traveling down a nearly deserted stretch of highway. With no more airplanes to catch, no more conflicting events to choose from, my thoughts started drifting back over my incredible year, which was about to end. I felt extremely fortunate that everything had worked out right, enabling me to realize my dream.

The most obvious thing that could have sidelined me was a blow to my health or the health of my family. Luckily, we all remained well. Also, I was fortunate that my business partners indulged my fantasy year. My long-time partners, my brother

Charles and the man whom my mother considers her third son, Pete Field, were especially accommodating. In recent years, we've been delighted and fortunate that our children have chosen to join us in the business as partners, assuming many of the responsibilities of day-to-day management: Charles' boys Chuck and Bill; Pete's son Robert; and my son Ed. All four of these young men are extremely capable and hard-working and, to their credit, they have all married bright, beautiful women and have lovely families.

As I allowed my thoughts to drift back over the year of my dreams, it was difficult to believe the sheer enormity of it all. Over the previous 12 months, I had traveled to all 50 states, seen all 50 state capitols and attended 250 sporting events (including games at all 28 Major League Baseball ballparks) while traveling more than 10,000 auto miles and 109,000 air miles, with 624 take offs and landings. Thank goodness, that was an even number! During the course of my travels, I bought approximately 500 souvenir t-shirts and about 750 souvenir ballcaps. I snapped over 150 rolls of film, which comes to more than 4,500 photographs.

Anyone who has traveled a great deal knows what a pain it can be at times, and on many occasions, I found myself irritated by the long lines at the ticket counters, security checkpoints, and sky-ways. Due to delays caused by weather and equipment failure, I found myself spending an inordinate amount of time waiting around airports, and there are only so many newspapers you can read in a given day. And how many times can you be asked: "Has anyone unknown to you asked you to carry an item on this flight?" and "Have any of the items you are traveling with been out of your immediate control since you packed them?" Ticket agents asked me these questions a total of 312 times throughout the year. There were times when I wanted to answer "yes!" just to see how they would react.

Two baggage issues agitated me tremendously. The way some passengers refuse to check anything amazed me. I can't tell you how many times I waited in line to get onto a plane while some inconsiderate person tried to stuff four hundred pounds of baggage into an overhead compartment. Or, if I had gotten on first, I invariably watched one of those people cram their bags into the same storage space as mine, squashing my poor defenseless briefcase in the process.

The other major irritant came at baggage claim. Why is it that all those people have to stand so close to the carousel, making bag retrieval a contact sport? The perfect solution for this problem is for the airports to place a line five feet away from the conveyer belt. When someone's bag appears, he or she may step up and retrieve it. That way, you don't have to feel like you're fighting your way through the jungle just to grab your Samsonite.

The increasingly impersonal nature of travel in this computer age also bothered me at times. Sometimes I found myself standing in front of a ticket agent who appeared to be ignoring me while typing away on a keyboard. I wanted to scream: "Is there a problem? Say something to me! Anything! Look at me! Talk to me!"

Mostly, though, the memories flooding through my mind that morning as I made my way toward Cramton Bowl were of the interesting places, people and sporting events that had made my journey such an adventure: The thrill (and fear) of The Idi-

---

tarod . . . The excitement of watching my friend Ellis Ferreira compete in the World Doubles Championships . . . The pleasure of seeing the men's and women's Final Four with my mother . . . The suspense of watching the seventh game of the World Series go into extra innings with our group from Birmingham . . . The nostalgic joy of seeing 47 of the 50 greatest NBA players of all time standing on the court at the 50th anniversary NBA All-Star Game . . . The patriotic pride of watching all those cadets and midshipmen take the field before the Army-Navy football game.

In many cases, my most enjoyable experiences had little or nothing to do with sports, but rather flowed from the natural course of traveling around this great country of ours and encountering the incredible diversity of places and people. My trip through New England was on my mind. One beautiful day in April, I drove from Hanover, New Hampshire (where I had attended a women's softball game between Dartmouth and Princeton the previous day) to the state capitol of Vermont in Montpelier, toured the ski and tennis resorts at Stowe, visited the Ben & Jerry's ice cream headquarters on the road to Burlington, and toured the University of Vermont campus where I caught a few innings of Vermont's baseball game against Sienna. At the capitol, I happened to meet a political reporter who told me about the Waybury Inn, a quaint little hotel in East Middleburg where they had filmed the exterior scenes for the television show "Newhart."

I couldn't believe my luck.

At this point, I feel the need to make a confession. I'm a big Bob Newhart fan. And Mary Tyler Moore. And Andy Griffith.

Late at night, when I find myself unable to sleep and can't find my new friend "the Black Widow" on ESPN, I often turn on Nick at Nite and watch the reruns of "The Bob Newhart Show" or "Newhart." So naturally, after discovering that I was within driving distance of the setting of the fictional Stratford Inn, I changed my plans for the evening and drove to East Middleburg, a beautiful village filled with antique shops, bed-and-breakfasts and renowned Middleburg College.

When I pulled up to the Waybury Inn and walked into the lobby, I halfway expected to be greeted by Joanna wearing a tight-fitting sweater or perhaps encounter Larry and his brother Darrell and his other brother Darrell!

The clerk was a nice middle-aged lady who didn't have to look into a computer screen to remember my reservation. In contrast to all those impersonal airline agents, she was warm and friendly and she didn't even have a computer. She had taken my reservation over the phone several hours before. "Oh, no," she had said politely "We don't need your credit card number. I'll save a room for you . . ." Believe me, that was the only time I had been told that!

They only had 14 rooms in the whole hotel and there was hardly anyone in the place.

As I checked in, the rare simplicity of the process still amazed me. When I checked in, the nice lady handed me the keys to three different rooms. "Go upstairs and see which one you like best," she advised.

So I walked up the stairs and inspected all three rooms. They were all about the same. None had televisions or telephones.

The furniture and bathroom fixtures looked like they had been lifted from a 50-year-old movie. I chose a room, and since there was nothing to do — ironically, this was the one hotel room I had ever stayed in where I couldn't watch "Newhart" — I wandered down to the lobby and inspected the glass case which housed numerous autographed photos and other mementos from the show. To my surprise, there was a restaurant with a separate lounge at the back of the hotel, and I wound up having a nice dinner and drinks in the lounge.

The place was full of locals and I struck up a conversation with an interesting young man who had worked on the homeless problem under the socialist mayor of Burlington, who is now Vermont's only congressman. As we watched an NHL playoff game on the bar's television, the young man and I had a fascinating conversation. It's not every day that an Alabama Republican gets the chance to spend several hours sharing drinks and ideas about politics and life with such a liberal in the most liberal state in America.

My night at the Waybury Inn proved to be one of the most relaxing evenings of the year, giving me a brief respite from the hustle and bustle of my sports tour.

One of the most rewarding things about my trip was getting to visit with several young people who had grown up with my children and were living in different parts of the country pursuing their own lives and careers as young adults. In San Francisco, I had dinner with Birmingham native Leigh Thomasson and her boyfriend Lawson Brown. The meal I had that night in June at the famed Fleur de Lys was the best of the entire year, and talking with them about how they were chasing their own dreams made the evening all the more fulfilling. In New York City, I got to have dinner and attend a New York Knicks-Miami Heat NBA playoff game with Jay McGehee, who was working on Wall Street. Jay is originally from Jackson, Mississippi, and had attended the University of Alabama with my daughter Ann. In Chicago, I went to a White Sox game and a Bulls-Heat playoff game with Lathrop Smith, who was a high school friend of Ann's. In Columbia, South Carolina, Birmingham native Caroline Brady LaMotte and her husband Bill were gracious hosts for dinner and South Carolina's overtime basketball victory over Kentucky.

In retrospect, I was amazed at having missed only one event that I had planned to see all year long. On my way back from Green Bay during the NFL regular season, having watched a noontime game between the Packers and the Buccaneers, I scheduled a three-hour layover in Chicago. I had never seen a game at storied Soldier Field, and the Bears were playing New Orleans, led by former Bears player and coach Mike Ditka, who was returning to Chicago for the first time as the head coach of the Saints. Upon arriving at O'Hare Airport, I caught a cab to Soldier Field, but got stuck in a massive traffic jam. It took me more than an hour to get to the stadium. Since I had no bags and no hotel reservations and faced an impending flight, I was afraid I would not be able to get another cab, so I never got out of the taxi. I had the taxi driver take me back to the airport and was frustrated to find out that my flight was delayed. Instead of watching a game at historic Soldier Field, I sat in the airport bar watching it on television.

The biggest humiliation of the entire year was the morning in Boston when I went downstairs from my room at the Ritz Carlton for breakfast and the maitre d' refused to seat me because I was wearing a University of Kentucky warm-up suit. I'm surprised he could see what I was wearing since his nose was so high in the air. He didn't seem impressed that C.M. Newton had personally given me that suit and that I had worn that suit at various times on my yearlong adventure.

Back in the late 1930s, a promoter named Champ Pickens devised the idea of launching an annual football all-star game in Montgomery pitting college seniors from the north against college seniors from the south. The first game was played on January 2, 1939 (a 6-0 victory by the north), and through the years, the Blue-Gray Game grew into Montgomery's most important sporting event. Each year, many of college football's greatest players end their college careers in front of the pro scouts at Cramton Bowl, making the game an important bridge between college and professional football. In 1997, National Football League rosters included 250 athletes who played in the Blue-Gray Game. Televised nationally on Christmas Day by ABC Sports, the game is always one of the highest rated college football games of the year, climbing as high as fifth among all the post-season games.

In 1955, the Montgomery Lions Club acquired the game and turned it into an important charitable event. Over the last four decades, the club has raised more than $3.5 million for charity, including $222,000 in 1997. The Lions Club uses the money for a variety of worthwhile causes, including testing all third graders in Montgomery County for vision problems.

When I arrived in Montgomery for the Blue-Gray Game, parked my car and walked across the street to the Cramton Bowl, the first person I ran into was Reese McKinney, who at the time was administrative assistant to Montgomery's infamous mayor, Emory Folmar. At this writing, Reese is probate judge of Montgomery County. After talking with Reese and his daughter Rebecca and wishing them a Merry Christmas, I took the two tickets my mother gave me and walked to my seat. As soon as I walked into the stadium, I encountered my lifelong friend Joe McInnes, and his daughter Missy. Joe and I had grown up together in Wetumpka, were roommates and fraternity brothers at the University of Alabama, and remain close friends to this day.

After sitting with Joe and Missy for the first quarter, I spotted former Elmore County Probate Judge Ed Enslen, his attorney son, John Enslen, who had played quarterback several years behind me at Wetumpka High School, and John's son-in-law and law partner, Patrick Pinkston. I sat with them for the second quarter and we had a good time catching up on Wetumpka gossip.

At halftime, I wandered around the stadium pestering the stew out of people. It seemed like every time I turned around I saw someone I knew, and I started wondering why none of those people had invited me to go to the game with them. Of course, it was inevitable that I would run into Mayor Folmar, who was in his element on his city's big day, and his wife Anita.

When the third quarter started, I went to sit with Dr. Steve Phelen and his wife Carolyn, whom I've known since college.

Their son, Stephen, had been a star athlete at Trinity School in Montgomery. He had just finished an outstanding academic and athletic playing career with the University of Virginia, and was honored to be selected as a defensive back on the Gray squad.

In the second quarter, this home-town boy intercepted a Blue pass, which turned out to be one of the highlights of the day for the highly partisan crowd, which celebrated a 31-24 Gray victory. Both Steve and Carolyn are still beaming with pride.

Because Alabama had finished 4-7 and failed to earn a bowl invitation for only the third time in four decades, the Blue-Gray Game took on greater significance with the presence of three Crimson Tide players: backs Dennis Riddle, Curtis Alexander and Ed Scissum. Thus, the Blue-Gray Game was like 'Bama's bowl game for 1997.

After the game, I walked to my car with mixed emotions. As I drove back to Birmingham, where Louise and the children were expecting me for our family Christmas, I was torn between the sense of accomplishment I felt in having achieved my goal and the profound regret that my magical year was over. For the first time in a year, I had no plane to worry about catching. No tickets to procure. No bags to pack. I have to admit, I felt a bit deflated.

I let my mind wander back through the year, lingering on the many talented athletic performances I had been so fortunate to witness and all the many interesting people and places I had encountered. It was natural to start wondering about how the trip had affected my life. It certainly had given me many wonderful memories that will always bring me pleasure and a sense of accomplishment. But it was bigger than that. My year on the road was a grand adventure in which I chased more than sporting events. I had pursued a childhood dream and, in the process, celebrated my life. On my way home from Montgomery, I knew that whatever happened to me in the future, I would not look back on my life and wonder what might have been. Even though I was wistful about the end of my trip, part of me had never felt so alive and empowered.

When I walked into my house late that afternoon for our family Christmas celebration, aglow in my accomplishment, Louise quickly pulled me back into my old/new reality. "Edgar," she said, "where have you been? We've been waiting on you!" ■

The world is a book,

and those who do not travel

read only one page.

— St. Augustine

APPENDIX I

Halls of Fame

I n previous years before my year-long sports adventure, I had visited the Baseball Hall of Fame in Cooperstown, New York, and the Basketball Hall of Fame in Springfield, Massachusetts. During my sports trip, I wanted to see as many additional halls of fame as possible.

In 1997 I visited:

- The College Football Hall of Fame
  South Bend, Indiana
- The Horse Racing Hall of Fame
  Saratoga Springs, New York
- The New England Sports Hall of Fame
  Boston, Massachusetts
- The Indianapolis Motor Speedway Hall of Fame
  Indianapolis, Indiana
- The Green Bay Packer Hall of Fame
  Green Bay, Wisconsin
- The Little League World Series Hall of Fame
  Williamsport, Pennsylvania
- The International Lawn Tennis Hall of Fame
  Newport, Rhode Island
- The Paul W. Bryant Museum
  Tuscaloosa, Alabama
- The Motorsports Hall of Fame
  Talledega, Alabama

I also toured non-sports museums:

- The Rock and Roll Hall of Fame
  Cleveland, Ohio
- The California State Railroad Museum
  Sacramento, California
- The Frontier Days Wild West Museum
  Cheyenne, Wyoming

I would challenge any state or regional Hall of Fame to match the inductees that are members of the Alabama Sports Hall of Fame located in Birmingham.

Some of our members, in no particular order: Joe Louis, Bart Starr, Bear Bryant, Shug Jordan, Jesse Owens, Joe Namath, Hank Aaron, Willie Mays, Gene Stallings, Jerry Pate, Bo Jackson, C.M. Newton, Lee Roy Jordan, Bobby and Davey Allison, Kenny Stabler, Pat Sullivan, John Stallworth, John Hannah, Dwight Stephenson, Ozzie Smith, Neil Bonnett, Bobby Bowden, Tommie Agee, LeRoy "Satchel" Page, and many other greats.

During my sports trip I returned to Birmingham for the Alabama Sports Hall of Fame 29th Annual Induction Ceremony. I was host for one of our new inductees, Birmingham native T.R. Dunn, who is a former University of Alabama Basketball standout and currently serves as an assistant coach in the NBA.

Larry Striplin, who served as Chairman of the Board for a number of years, and Executive Director Bill Legg, led the effort to build a first rate facility to showcase these great sports legends. This is the finest state or regional Sports Hall of Fame in America.

Recently, the Alabama Sports Hall of Fame Board and its staff, under the leadership of Chairman Richard Scrushy and President Dr. Gaylon McCollough, began involving former inductees to help raise the level of awareness and showcase the possibilities that sports can offer. These special marketing and outreach programs as motivational influences are directed especially toward the school-age children of Alabama.

The inspiration of two of the original inductees, Alabama's Coach Paul "Bear" Bryant and Auburn's Coach Ralph "Shug" Jordan inspired Larry Striplin to create and bring to fruition a nationally recognized high school awards program — The Bryant-Jordan Student-Athlete Scholarship Program. The money raised to endow this scholarship fund will provide outstanding Alabama high school senior boys and girls an opportunity to pursue college degrees for generations to come.

This program is ably promoted and coordinated by Wetumpka native, Executive Director Ken Blankenship — whom I consider to be the second best quarterback to ever come out of Wetumpka High School!

I would like to extend to you, the reader, an invitation to visit and see for yourself what the Alabama Sports Hall of Fame in Birmingham has to offer. ∎

APPENDIX II

Some Great Characters . . .

I n my travels, some of the greatest surprises were the people I met. Here are a few more of the nice and interesting people I met along the way — some of whom I still hear from.

- When at the University of Connecticut I was escorted to the president's home by U of C Campus Police Officer, Peter Tanaka.

- In Tuscaloosa for the NCAA Regional Baseball Championship, my friend and former neighbor, Russell Stutts (another big 'Bama fan) and I met and got to know and visit with Jonathan Kotler, Dean of the Graduate School at the University of Southern California. His son, John, was batboy for USC and they were at the Capstone for four days for the Baseball Championship.

- At the 2nd game of the NBA Finals in Chicago, Bulls vs Utah Jazz, I sat next to Tim Gauer. We visited during the game. He was well-informed and answered all my questions. I learned that the two tickets I had purchased from a broker were two of Tim's four tickets. After the game I asked Tim about a ticket if I decided to return for the Finals as it would be a better deal for both of us. Next game, Tim, who lived in the suburbs and who was not attending the game that night, drove into downtown and personally delivered the tickets to me.

- While attending the WPA World Nine-Ball Championship in Chicago, I met Paul Gerni, who is the World Trick Shot Champion from Shawnee, Kansas. We discussed the possibility of his coming to Birmingham to put on an exhibition at the Mountain Brook Inn. And sure enough — a year later — Paul has performed at the Mountain Brook Inn to rave reviews.

- The day I toured the capitol in Augusta, Maine, I was out on the third floor balcony with large rocking chairs where you can relax and enjoy the view. There I began talking to the only other two people touring. They were Clayton and Mary Sullivan of Hattiesburg, Mississippi. They knew Lauren Welden, who is married to my nephew Chuck. Lauren is a native of Hattiesburg and had babysat their children!

- On my flight home from the NAIA Basketball Tournament in Tulsa, I met Terry Swartz, who works for Nike in sports marketing. When we arrived in Birmingham, we watched the ending of one of the NCAA Playoff games on the television in the airport bar. We continued talking and I ended up driving him to the Mountain Brook Inn. When we arrived, Coach Lute Olson and his wife were in the hotel lobby where we made photos with them. Turned out Terry is friends with the athletic director at Arizona, and we later got together with him.

- At a pre-game party in Lincoln, before the Nebraska-Kansas State football game, I met Kerry Kearl, who works for a friend of mine, Duane Acklie, who was my host for the weekend. Kerry told me that his daughter, Cheyenne, a high school honor student, was considering attending the University of Alabama School of Communication. As this book is being written, Cheyenne, who received many scholarship offers, is in fact a coed at the University in Tuscaloosa.

- One beautiful day on the campus of the University of Providence, Providence, Rhode Island, I was watching a softball game and on an adjoining field, watching a lacrosse match. I struck up a conversation with Steve Robertson, another sports fan. I was amazed as he talked. He was a wealth of information about his state's history, politics and sports. Then he began talking about Alabama and I was surprised that he was so knowledgeable about Alabama sports. We have corresponded several times.

- While at the Ironman on the island of Kona, I met Brian and Lesley Bayliss of Stockton, Australia. Their daughter, Kelly, who is a physical therapist, was a competitor. We were standing together talking when she came from the swim, jumped on her bike and took off on the second leg. Brian and Lesley invited me to visit them if I make it to the 2000 Olympics.

- Also visiting with us were Dick and Priscilla Dresie of Kailua-Kona, Hawaii. Dick is a travel coordinator with Alii Travel. They also sell Christmas ornaments all over the Pacific. In years past, Dick and Priscilla have worked as volunteers for the Ironman competition, so it was really interesting talking to them about the event, and its history.

- I was looking for a ticket to the Angels vs Oakland A's game and met Phil Berg outside the stadium. It is illegal to sell tickets outside the gate, and so he took me inside and then I paid him regular price for the ticket. He lives in Anaheim but is originally from Michigan. My seat was next to his so we talked about sports and family. He has three sons and all are big sports fans. One son attends Arizona and plays club ice hockey, and one who had attended Michigan State was coming back to California to pursue a career in modeling. His other son went to Kentucky. After the game, I tried to get him to go across the street with me to Arrowhead Pond, the stadium that Disney owns, where the Anaheim Ducks of the National Hockey League play. That night they were having a roller hockey game. Phil is a big hockey fan and thought it a sacrilege to play or watch roller hockey — a purist of the game.

- In Los Angeles, for the First Women's National Basketball Association game, I sat by and talked with Paula Silver who is with Interscope Productions in Los Angeles. She had brought her daughter and some of her daughter's friends to the game. Paula was really proud as we talked about women finally having a pro league sponsored by the NBA which will ensure the WNBA success and afford girls the opportunity to play professional ball in the USA. Paula, her friends and all the girls were a part of the "Card Show" with signs spelling out LESLIE. I was also given a letter — so each time Lisa Leslie, former USC player, now a star for the LA Sparks, would score, we all stood up and held our signs high. Paula was getting ready to go to Montana and work on a movie with Robin Williams.

- At the Kick-off Classic in East Rutherford, New Jersey, I sat next to Mike Mangold, who is a detective from Marlton, New Jersey. Mike was the guest of Robbie Reid who had been one of his teammates when they played basketball at Rutgers in the mid '70s. Reid's nephew is Ron Dayne, star running back of the Badgers. The game was between the Syracuse Orangemen and the Wisconsin Badgers. Mike was on the TV Show "America's Most Wanted" the next week talking about one of his cases. A man he had previously arrested was being named to the Ten Most Wanted List. Mike had worked some cases involving the guy in the past. At this writing, the bank robber has been apprehended. Mike was wearing a big championship ring and I asked him about it. He told me how he had been a trainer for former WBA Heavyweight Champion of the World, Bruce Seldon. Seldon became champion in 1995 by defeating Tony Tucker. Mike Tyson beat Seldon in '96 and then Evander Holyfield beat Tyson.

- In Honolulu when I visited the Kamaka ukulele factory, I met a young man, Kekoa Eskaran of Kamaeul, Hawaii. Kekoa was there with his family to tour the factory and to purchase a ukulele for his birthday. We talked during our tour and Kekoa told me that his team had come close to qualifying for the Little League World Series which I had attended. I asked him to send me the follow-up newspaper articles about the Ironman. He did and I sent him a World Series ballcap and t-shirt.

- While in Philadelphia for a Flyers vs Rangers NHL Playoff game, I met Jim Genuardi, Sr. of Norristown, Pennsylvania.

We were talking and Jim told me that he had nine brothers and sisters. He and four of his brothers and now their sons are in the grocery business — Genuardi's Family Market. His fifth brother is a priest. His story reminded me of Vic; I told him that my father was one of ten children also — the make-up just the opposite of Jim's as my father was one of four boys, and that Vic had also been in the grocery business. I enjoyed our conversation. Their family market is one of the sponsors of the Flyers hockey team.

- When in Boston for the NFL Playoff game and college basketball, I was touring the historical district and at noon I went into a little Italian restaurant for lunch. Two couples came in and sat at the next table. We began talking and they asked where I was from (guess I don't have a Boston accent!) and I told them Birmingham, Alabama. Their car was parked outside and they were packed to leave right after lunch to drive to Auburn University where Troy Bland had a brother in school. They were members of a band — Sun House Band — and after their visit in Auburn would be driving to San Francisco to promote their music.

- At the baggage claim in Columbia, South Carolina, I met Dennis Duffy, who is a coal broker from Georgia, formerly of Kentucky. We were talking about the basketball game and I asked him about tickets. He said he had a buddy he was meeting later who might have an extra ticket. Later I went over to his hotel — The Adams Mark — where I saw him in the bar with friends. They did not have an extra ticket for me, but while we were visiting there, some people with a Lexington, Kentucky, TV Station asked if we would hold up some Wild-cat shakers and do some cheering for Kentucky for them to transmit live for the 6:00 news. We did it. ■

APPENDIX III

Welden's Lists

N*o rules, no rhyme, no reason other than my own personal thoughts and opinions....*

I saw games at 28 major league ballparks
and offer the following:

■ **Best Old Stadiums**
- Wrigley Field   Chicago
- Fenway Park   Boston
- Tiger Stadium   Detroit

■ **Best New Stadiums**
- Camden Yard   Baltimore
- Turner Field   Atlanta
- Jacobs Field   Cleveland

■ **Best Dome Stadiums**
- SkyDome   Toronto
- Hubert H. Humphrey Metrodome   Minneapolis

■ **Stadiums with the Friendliest and Most Helpful Employees**
- Hubert H. Humphrey Metrodome — Minneapolis
- Busch Stadium — St. Louis
- Kauffman Stadium — Kansas City
- Veterans Stadium — Philadelphia

■ **Of the Professional Football Games I Attended, My Choices as the Best Stadiums**
- Ericsson Stadium — Charlotte
- Jack Kent Cooke Stadium — Washington, DC
- Jacksonville Municipal Stadium — Jacksonville

■ **Best College Stadiums**
- University of Michigan — Ann Arbor
- Ohio State University — Columbus
- University of Nebraska — Lincoln

■ **Most Impressive College Campuses**
- Princeton University — Princeton, N.J.
- United States Military Academy — West Point, N.Y.
- University of Virginia — Charlottesville

■ **Most Exciting College Football Games**
- Georgia vs Georgia Tech — Atlanta
- Ohio State vs Arizona State — Rose Bowl, Pasadena
- Michigan vs Notre Dame — Ann Arbor

■ **Most Inspirational Athletes**
- Brett Favre
- DeeDee Jonrowe
- Joe Reddington, Sr.
- Members of the wheelchair basketball teams

■ **Best Performance by an Athlete**
- Michael Jordan
- Randy Moss

■ **Best Team Effort**
- Green Bay defeats San Francisco in NFL Playoff game
- North Carolina State defeats Duke in ACC Basketball Tournament

■ **Best Pre-game or Half-time Entertainment**
- Ohio State Marching Band

■ **Gutsiest Comeback**
- Mexico at the Little League World Series

■ **Most Exciting Events**
- The Iditarod and the Iditaride
- The "Start" of the Indy 500
- Being on the sideline at 2 NFL games

- **Loudest Crowds**
  - Cameron Indoor Stadium — Durham, N.C.
    Duke defeating North Carolina in college basketball
  - Joe Louis Arena — Detroit
    Detroit Red Wings defeating Philadelphia Flyers
    Stanley Cup final game

- **Pro Sports' Big Championships' Clinching Games in Order of Excitement**
  - Hockey   Detroit Red Wings defeating
               Philadelphia Flyers
  - Basketball Chicago Bulls defeating Utah Jazz
  - Baseball   Florida Marlins defeating Cleveland Indians
  - Football   The SuperBowl: Green Bay Packers defeating
               New England Patriots

- **Most Exciting College Basketball Games**
  Regular Season
  - Kentucky at South Carolina
    South Carolina wins in overtime
  - North Carolina at Duke
    Duke defeats Carolina
  - Arizona at Florida State
    FSU wins in Tallahassee

  Tournaments
  - Arizona & Kentucky NCAA Finals
    Arizona wins championship in overtime
  - Providence & Arizona Regional Finals
    Arizona wins in overtime in Birmingham

- NCAA Women's Final Four
  Old Dominion defeats Stanford in semi-finals

■ **Most Unusual Sporting Events I attended**
  - X Games
  - Lumberjack Competition
  - Roller Hockey
  - Ultimate Fighting

■ **Most Expensive Tickets**
  - Stanley Cup Playoffs — Final Game
    Detroit defeats Philadelphia
  - Holyfield - Tyson Fight in Las Vegas
    Holyfield wins - Tyson draws blood with teeth
  - NBA All Star Game — 50th Anniversary

■ **Fewest Tickets Available at Any Price**
  - Masters Golf Tournament — Augusta, Ga.
  - Duke vs North Carolina — Cameron Indoor Stadium

■ **Very Special Events I Witnessed**
  - North Carolina's Coach Dean Smith breaking
    Adolph Rupp's record
  - 50th Anniversary of Jackie Robinson breaking
    baseball's color barrier
  - Pre-Season College Football Game Honoring the
    Winningest Coach, Eddie Robinson of Grambling,
    upon his retirement, with proceeds going to support
    black coaches

■ **"First Evers" I Attended**

- 1st Women's WNBA Game
  Los Angeles vs New York, Los Angeles

- 1st Major Inter League Baseball Game
  Texas Rangers vs S.F. Giants, Arlington

- 1st Game at Jack Kent Cooke Stadium
  Washington vs Arizona, Washington DC

- 1st Game at Turner Field
  Atlanta vs Chicago Cubs, Atlanta

- 1st Game with Rick Pitino coaching the Celtics
  Boston vs Chicago, Boston

- 1st Two-Piece Swimsuit Competition
  Miss America, Atlantic City

■ **"Last Evers" I Attended**

- Last game for North Carolina Coach Dean Smith.
  North Carolina loses to Arizona in Semi-finals of
  NCAA Final Four

- Last college game for Kentucky Coach Rick Pitino
  before leaving for the NBA Boston Celtics. Kentucky
  loses to Arizona in finals of NCAA Final Four.

- Last home hockey game of National Hockey League
  Star Mario Lemieux at Pittsburgh

■ **Most Exciting Events Where I Had a Personal Interest**

- Alabama defeats Southern California in the
  Regional Finals to win a slot in the College
  Baseball World Series

- Alabama defeats Miami twice in the College Baseball World Series
- Birmingham Southern wins the first two rounds in close games at the NAIA Basketball Championship in Tulsa
- John Zimmerman and his partner finish 3rd in the U.S. National Skating Championship qualifying for a place in the World Skating Championship

■ **Temperature Changes**
Coldest Events
- Green Bay vs San Francisco Play-off Game in Green Bay
- The Iditarod in Anchorage
- Army vs Navy Football Game at The Meadowlands

Hottest Events
- Florida vs Tennessee Football Game, Gainesville
- Lipton Tennis Tournament, Miami
- Baseball - College World Series, Omaha

■ **Favorite Airport**
- Tampa

■ **Least Favorite Airport**
- Cincinnati

■ **Best Lodging**
- Lafayette Park Hotel   Lafayette, California
- Four Seasons Hotel   Chicago, Illinois
- Keswick   Charlottesville, Virginia
- Turnberry Resort   Fort Lauderdale, Florida

■ **Worst Lodging**
- Budget Lodge   Gainesville, Florida

■ **Special Non-Sporting Events**
- My daughter's wedding
- Touring around — Boise, Sun Valley, Helena, Jackson Hole, Yellowstone National Park and Old Faithful
- July 4th Cruise — from Seattle up to Victoria
- Overnight at the Waybury Inn
- Trip to Juneau — helicoptered onto an ice glacier and walked around; went salmon fishing and whale & eagle watching

■ **State Capitals** — I visited all fifty.
(Listed in random order)

Favorites	Least Favorites
• New Hampshire	• New Jersey
• Vermont	• Louisiana
• Indiana	• New Mexico
• South Dakota	• Arizona
• Texas	• Tennessee
• Mississippi	• Alaska
• Utah	• Hawaii

■

APPENDIX IV

Traveling . . .

I was lucky. With all the miles I flew and drove, I really had few problems. I couldn't have breakfast at the Ritz Carlton in Boston because I was wearing my Kentucky warm-up suit. On one trip to Chicago the hotel had over booked. I left my driver's license in South Hampton but thanks to my secretary, I could still rent a car and fly. I had an airline ticket to Charleston, South Carolina, when I was really going to Charleston, West Virginia — my luggage went on to South Carolina. I left my small leather bag that I took everywhere under my seat at The Preakness; I called and they retrieved it and promptly mailed it to me. Once I thought I had lost my cell phone — after calling all the airports I had passed through, I found it hidden in the corner of my briefcase. I fit some sort of profile that sent up a red flag to airport security so I was searched several times. I think it must have been because I seldom had a round-trip ticket. In all the travel, I can remember losing my temper three times — at the Puerto Rican Shoot-out over tickets, at the train station in Princeton, New Jersey, with a fellow customer who unnecessarily stuck his nose in my business, and then in New York at a play where I had a run-in with a smart-alec vendor over a diet-coke — I hate diet drinks.

PACKING

■ Ed gave me a leather Hartman expandable briefcase for Christmas the day before my trip began. I kept it full with:
- Calendar of events
- Different sporting schedules
- Newspapers and magazines
- Business related items
- Mountain Smith Accessory Pouch (5"x12") made of soft leather given to me by Ann

■ I took the accessory pouch with me to all the games. It contained:
- Sunglasses
- Pens
- Business cards
- Sunscreen
- Cameras (Samsung Maxima Zoom & Pentax IQZoom 115m)
- Film (200 & 400 speed Kodak, 24 & 36 exposures)
- Tape recorder - Sony VOR
- Maxell MC Gour tapes
- Cell phone

■ Suitcase:
Soft-side bag that I always checked! Never did I carry my suitcase on board the aircraft. I did not use a hanging suit bag. I learned to fold everything neatly into one bag. Sometimes, if I overbought souvenirs at games, that bag got really

stuffed. I wore a pair of shoes and packed one pair — tennis shoes and dress shoes. I packed mostly casual clothes — khakis, sport shirts, and a sweater; however, I always took a sport coat, shirt and tie — just in case I needed them.

■ I became a "frequent flyer" with most airlines and benefited from some of their programs.

■ I took two credit cards — NBC MasterCard and American Express card and except for once, I always had my driver's license. I have the honor of serving on the Board of the National Bank of Commerce who issued my credit card. Their professional staff was most accommodating and helpful during my year of travel.

INTERIM TRIPS HOME

■ Film would go to Wolf Camera and Video to be developed. I would mail the snapshots to people I had met and write them a note.

■ My tapes would be transcribed and my events would be placed on a calendar/spreadsheet.

■ Plans for my next trip would be tied down or decided on. Ann was constantly doing research for upcoming events. We put together a large file box for each of the twelve months. Inside are expandable files with each day of the month labeled. All the ticket stubs, programs, newspaper articles covering the event, the photographs taken that day and my transcribed notes are in those files.

NOW THAT IT IS OVER, WHAT IS LEFT TO DO . . .

■ Share my story with various groups at civic club meetings and functions, and publish this book.

■ I plan to frame all the ticket stubs — by categories: championship games, regular season baseball tickets, football tickets, etc.

■ I hope to find a way to display the programs — especially those that are really great looking!

■ As for all those baseball caps —
Louise made me store them.
Excessive — I think that's the word she used.

Welden's Calendar of Events

Date	City	Activity

DECEMBER 1996

Date	City	Activity
26 Dec	Sacramento	NBA *Sacramento vs. Vancouver*
27 Dec	Sacramento	Toured the California State Capitol
27 Dec	Santa Clara	College Basketball Cable Car Classic *Alabama vs. San Jose State* *Detroit vs. Santa Clara*
28 Dec	Santa Clara	College Basketball Cable Car Classic *Alabama vs. Santa Clara*

JANUARY 1997

Date	City	Activity
1 Jan	Pasadena	Rose Bowl Parade Rose Bowl Game *Ohio St. vs. Arizona State*
2 Jan	New Orleans	Sugar Bowl *Florida vs. Florida State*
4 Jan	Green Bay	NFL Playoff game *Green Bay vs. San Francisco*

Date	City	Activity
5 Jan	Charlotte	NFL Playoff game *Charlotte vs. Dallas*
12 Jan	Foxboro	NFL Playoff game *New England vs. Jacksonville*
13 Jan	Boston	Toured Massachusetts State Capitol
13 Jan	Boston	College Basketball *Boston College vs. Georgetown*
13 Jan	Boston	NHL *Boston vs. Ottawa*
14 Jan	Boston	NBA *Boston vs. Golden State*
15 Jan	Chapel Hill	College Basketball *North Carolina vs.* *North Carolina State*
20 Jan	Birmingham	High School Basketball *Mountain Brook vs. West End*
22 Jan	Tuscaloosa	College Basketball *Alabama vs. South Carolina*
25 Jan	Birmingham	College Basketball *Alabama-Birmingham vs.* *Memphis*
25 Jan	Tuscaloosa	College Basketball *Alabama vs. Louisiana State*
26 Jan	New Orleans	NFL Super Bowl *Green Bay vs. New England*
29 Jan	Durham	College Basketball *Duke vs. North Carolina*

Date	City	Activity

FEBRUARY 1997

Date	City	Activity
3 Feb	Birmingham	College Basketball *Samford vs. Jacksonville State*
4 Feb	Columbia	Toured outside of the South Carolina State Capitol (due to construction)
4 Feb	Columbia	College Basketball *South Carolina vs. Kentucky*
5 Feb	Winston-Salem	College Basketball *Wake Forest vs. Duke*
6 Feb	Cincinnati	College Basketball *Cincinnati vs. Tulane*
7 Feb	Columbus	Toured the Ohio State Capitol
8 Feb	Cleveland	NBA All-Star Rookie Game
9 Feb	Cleveland	Toured Pro Football Hall of Fame in Canton
9 Feb	Cleveland	NBA 50th Anniversary All-Star Game
11 Feb	Bloomington	College Basketball *Indiana vs. Penn State*
12 Feb	West Lafayette	College Basketball *Purdue vs. Minnesota*
13 Feb	Indianapolis	Toured the Indiana State Capitol
14 Feb	Nashville	Toured the Tennessee State Capitol
14 Feb	Nashville	United States National Skating Championship

Date	City	Activity
16 Feb	Daytona	NASCAR *Daytona 500*
16 Feb	Gainesville	Women's College Basketball *Florida vs. Alabama*
17 Feb	Tampa	NHL *Tampa Bay vs. Detroit*
19 Feb	Tuscaloosa	College Baseball *Alabama vs. Louisiana Tech*
19 Feb	Tuscaloosa	College Basketball *Alabama vs. Kentucky*
22 Feb	Birmingham	Alabama Sports Hall of Fame Induction Banquet
23 Feb	Birmingham	Professional Rodeo
25 Feb	Birmingham	High School Basketball Alabama High School Championships (8 games)
26 Feb	Portland	NBA *Portland vs. New York*

MARCH 1997

Date	City	Activity
1 Mar	Anchorage	The Iditaride Sled Race Pre-Start
2 Mar	Anchorage	The Iditarod Sled Race
6 Mar	Memphis	College Basketball SEC Tournament *Vanderbilt vs. Mississippi State* *Alabama vs. Florida* *Auburn vs. Tennessee*

Date	City	Activity
7 Mar	Greensboro	College Basketball ACC Tournament *Maryland vs. Clemson* *North Carolina State vs. Duke* *North Carolina vs. Virginia* *Florida State vs. Wake Forest*
8 Mar	Greensboro	College Basketball ACC Tournament *North Carolina State vs. Maryland* *North Carolina vs. Wake Forest*
14 Mar	Charlotte	College Basketball NCAA Tournament Eastern Regional *Georgia vs. Chattanooga* *Illinois vs. Southern California* *Providence vs. Marquette* *Duke vs. Murray State*
15 Mar	Winston-Salem	College Basketball NCAA Tournament Eastern Regional *North Carolina vs. Colorado* *California vs. Villanova*
16 Mar	Tuscaloosa	Women's College Basketball *Alabama vs. St. Joseph*
18 Mar	Oklahoma City	Toured the Oklahoma State Capitol

Date	City	Activity
19 Mar	Tulsa	College Basketball NAIA Tournament Attended 4 games including: *Birmingham Southern vs. Masters*
20 Mar	Tulsa	College Basketball NAIA Tournament Attended 3 games including: *Birmingham Southern vs.* *Southeast Oklahoma*
21 Mar	Birmingham	College Basketball NCAA Tournament Southeast Regional Semi-Final *Kansas vs. Arizona* *Tennessee-Chattanooga vs.* *Providence*
22 Mar	Indianapolis	High School Basketball Indiana High School Boy's Basketball Semi-Finals *Delta vs. LaPorte* *North Bloomington vs. Kokomo*
22 Mar	Indianapolis	High School Basketball Indiana High School Boy's Basketball Final *North Bloomington vs. Delta*
23 Mar	Birmingham	College Basketball NCAA Tournament Southeast Regional Final *Arizona vs. Providence*
25 Mar	Miami	Lipton's Tennis Tournament
26 Mar	Miami	Lipton's Tennis Tournament

Date	City	Activity
26 Mar	Miami	NBA *Miami vs. Sacremento*
28 Mar	Cincinnati	Women's College Basketball NCAA Final Four Semi-Final *Stanford vs. Old Dominion* *Tennessee vs. Notre Dame*
29 Mar	Indianapolis	College Basketball NCAA Final Four Semi-Final *North Carolina vs. Arizona* *Kentucky vs. Minnesota*
30 Mar	Cincinnati	Women's College Basketball NCAA Final Four Final *Tennessee vs. Old Dominion*
31 Mar	Indianapolis	College Basketball NCAA Final Four Final *Arizona vs. Kentucky*

APRIL 1997

Date	City	Activity
4 Apr	Atlanta	Toured the Georgia State Capitol
4 Apr	Atlanta	MLB Opening Ceremony for Turner Stadium *Atlanta vs. Chicago (Cubs)*
5 Apr	Birmingham	Championship Wheelchair Basketball Game
9 Apr	Birmingham	College Baseball *Alabama vs. Alabama-Birmingham*
10 Apr	Augusta	Masters Golf Tournament

Date	City	Activity
13 Apr	Auburn	College Baseball *Auburn vs. Alabama*
15 Apr	New York	MLB 50th Anniversary Honoring Jackie Robinson *Los Angeles vs. New York (Mets)*
16 Apr	Birmingham	College Baseball *Samford vs. Alabama*
17 Apr	Gainesville	NCAA Women's Gymnastics Championship
18 Apr	Princeton	College Tennis *Princeton vs. Dartmouth*
19 Apr	New York	NFL College Draft
19 Apr	New York	NHL Stanley Cup Playoffs *New Jersey vs. Montreal*
20 Apr	Providence	Girls Softball *Providence vs. Holy Cross*
20 Apr	Providence	Lacrosse *Providence vs. Maryland Shoreline*
20 Apr	Foxboro	World Cup Soccer *United States vs. Mexico*
21 Apr	Trenton	Toured the New Hampshire State Capitol

Date	City	Activity
21 Apr	Boston	MLB *Boston vs. Baltimore*
21 Apr	Boston	Boston Marathon
21 Apr	Hanover	College Softball *Princeton vs. Dartmouth*
22 Apr	Montpelier	Toured the Vermont State Capitol
22 Apr	Burlington	College Baseball *Vermont vs. Sienna-New York*
23 Apr	Pittsburgh	NHL Stanley Cup Playoffs *Pittsburgh vs. Philadelphia*

MAY 1997

Date	City	Activity
2 May	Birmingham	Senior PGA Bruno's Memorial Classic
3 May	Louisville	Kentucky Derby
4 May	Atlanta	MLB *Atlanta vs. Pittsburgh*
4 May	Atlanta	NBA *Atlanta vs. Detroit*
5 May	Las Vegas	World Series of Poker
6 May	Salt Lake City	Toured the Utah State Capitol
6 May	Salt Lake City	NBA Playoffs *Utah vs. Los Angeles (Lakers)*

Date	City	Activity
7 May	Houston	NBA Playoffs *Houston vs. Seattle*
7 May	Houston	MLB *Houston vs. New York (Mets)*
11 May	Tuscaloosa	College Baseball *Alabama vs. Louisiana State*
12 May	New York	NBA Playoffs *New York vs. Miami*
16 May	Washington D.C.	Corel Masters Tennis Tournament
17 May	Baltimore	Preakness
18 May	Philadelphia	NHL Playoffs *Philadelphia vs. New York (Rangers)*
18 May	Philadelphia	MLB *Philadelphia vs. Houston*
19 May	Trenton	Toured the New Jersey State Capitol
19 May	Detroit	NHL Playoffs *Detroit vs. Colorado*
20 May	Lansing	Toured the Michigan State Capitol
20 May	Chicago	NBA Playoffs *Chicago vs. Miami*
22 May	Tuscaloosa	College Baseball NCAA Regional Championships *Alabama vs. Troy State* *Southern California vs. Virginia Tech*

Date	City	Activity
23 May	Tuscaloosa	College Baseball NCAA Regional Championships *Alabama vs. Wichita State* *Southern California vs. Troy State*
24 May	Birmingham	Turkey Tennis Tournament
24 May	Tuscaloosa	College Baseball NCAA Regional Championships *Alabama vs.* *North Carolina State*
25 May	Tuscaloosa	College Baseball NCAA Regional Championship *Alabama vs. Southern California*
26 May	Indianapolis	Indianapolis 500
28 May	Montgomery	Toured Alabama State Capitol
28 May	Montgomery	College Baseball NCAA Division II Baseball Championships *Tampa vs. Southern Illinois*

JUNE 1997

Date	City	Activity
2 June	Omaha	College Baseball NCAA World Series *Alabama vs. Miami* *Mississippi State vs. UCLA*
3 June	Lincoln	Toured the Nebraska State Capitol

Date	City	Activity
3 June	Omaha	College Baseball NCAA World Series *Auburn vs. Stanford* *Alabama vs. Mississippi State*
4 June	Chicago	NBA Finals *Chicago vs. Utah*
5 June	Omaha	College Baseball NCAA World Series *Alabama vs. Miami*
6 June	Omaha	College Baseball NCAA World Series *Alabama vs. Miami*
7 June	Omaha	College Baseball NCAA World Series *Alabama vs. Louisiana State*
7 June	Detroit	NHL Stanley Cup Finals *Detroit vs. Philadelphia*
11 June	Birmingham	Minor League Baseball Rickwood Classic *Birmingham vs. Chattanooga*
12 June	Dallas	MLB *Texas vs. San Francisco*
13 June	Chicago	MLB *Chicago (Cubs) vs. Milwaukee*

Date	City	Activity
13 June	Chicago	NBA Finals *Chicago vs. Utah*
14 June	Washington D.C.	USGA — United States Open Golf Tournament
21 June	Los Angeles	WNBA Inaugural Game *Los Angeles vs. New York*
21 June	Los Angeles	MLB *California vs. Oakland*
21 June	Los Angeles	Roller Hockey *St. Louis Vipers vs.* *Anaheim Bullfrogs*
22 June	San Diego	MLB *San Diego vs. Colorado*
22 June	San Diego	X-Games
23 June	San Diego	X-Games
24 June	Los Angeles	MLB *Los Angeles vs. Colorado*
25 June	San Francisco	MLB *San Francisco vs. San Diego*
26 June	Oakland	MLB *Oakland vs. Texas*
28 June	Las Vegas	World Boxing Heavy Weight Championship *Holyfield vs. Tyson*
30 June	Salem	Toured the Oregon State Capitol

Date	City	Activity

JULY 1997

Date	City	Activity
1 July	Olympia	Toured the Washington State Capitol
1 July	Olympia	MLB *Seattle vs. San Francisco*
2 July	Juneau	Toured the Alaska State Capitol
3 July	Juneau	Salmon Fishing
8 July	Cleveland	MLB 1997 All-Star Game
9 July	Newport	Hall of Fame Tennis Championship
10 July	Providence	Toured the Rhode Island State Capitol
14 July	Cincinnati	MLB *Cincinnati vs. St. Louis*
15 July	Topeka	Toured the Kansas State Capitol
15 July	Kansas City	MLB *Kansas City vs. Milwaukee*
16 July	Jefferson City	Toured the Missouri State Capitol
16 July	St. Louis	MLB *St. Louis vs. San Diego*
17 July	Springfield	Toured the Illinois State Capitol
18 July	Cleveland	MLB *Cleveland vs. Boston*

Date	City	Activity
21 July	Madison	Toured the Wisconsin State Capitol
21 July	Milwaukee	MLB *Milwaukee vs.* *New York (Yankees)*
22 July	St. Paul	Toured the Minnesota State Capitol
22 July	Minneapolis	MLB *Minnesota vs. Kansas City*
24 July	Montgomery	Girls High School Volleyball Alabama All-Star Game *North vs. South*
24 July	Montgomery	Girls High School Softball Alabama All-Star Game *North vs. South* (Slow Pitch) *North vs. South* (Fast Pitch)
25 July	Montgomery	High School Basketball Alabama All-Star Game *North vs. South* (Boys) *North vs. South* (Girls)
26 July	Montgomery	High School Baseball Alabama All-Star Game *North vs. South* (2 games)
27 July	Birmingham	Ultimate Fighting Championships
30 July	Miami	MLB *Florida vs. Cincinnati*
31 July	Nashville	National Swimming Championships

Date	City	Activity

AUGUST 1997

4 Aug   Pittsburgh   MLB
    Pittsburgh vs. Atlanta

5 Aug   Harrisburg   Toured the Pennsylvania
State Capitol

7 Aug   Pell City   Bass Masters Fishing Tournament
Launch

7 Aug   Tuscaloosa   Bryant Stamp Presentation

7 Aug   Birmingham   Bass Masters Fishing Tournament
Weigh In

8 Aug   Boise   Toured the Idaho
State Capitol

9 Aug   Sun Valley   Olympic Ice Skating Exhibition

9 Aug   Sun Valley   Trap Shooting

10 Aug   Helena   Minor League Rookie Baseball
    Helena vs. Butte

11 Aug   Helena   Toured the Montana
State Capitol

15 Aug   Cheyenne   Toured the Wyoming
State Capitol

15 Aug   Denver   Toured the Colorado
State Capitol

15 Aug   Denver   United States Gymnastics
Competition

Date	City	Activity
15 Aug	Denver	Major League Soccer *Colorado vs.* *New York/New Jersey*
15 Aug	Denver	MLB *Colorado vs. New York (Mets)*
19 Aug	Augusta	Toured the Maine State Capitol
21 Aug	Long Island	Huggy Bear Tennis Tournament
22 Aug	Long Island	Walburn's-Hamlet Cup Tennis Tournament
22 Aug	New York	USTA - United States Open Qualifying Matches
22 Aug	Williamsport	Little League Baseball Little League All-Star Game *USA vs. International Team*
23 Aug	Williamsport	Little League Baseball Little League World Series Game *California vs. Mexico*
24 Aug	New York	College Football Kickoff Classic *Syracuse vs. Wisconsin*
24 Aug	New York	WNBA *New York vs. Cleveland*
25 Aug	Albany	Toured the New York State Capitol
25 Aug	Saratoga	Saratoga Horse Race

Date	City	Activity
28 Aug	Columbus	College Football *Ohio State vs. Wyoming*
29 Aug	New York	USTA United States Open Tennis Tournament
30 Aug	New York	MLB *New York (Yankees) vs.* *Montreal*
31 Aug	New York	NFL *New York (Giants) vs.* *Philadelphia*

SEPTEMBER 1997

Date	City	Activity
2 Sep	Providence	75 & Over Nalon Grass Court Tennis Tournament
4 Sep	Charlottesville	College Football *Virginia vs. Auburn*
5 Sep	Richmond	Toured the Virginia State Capitol
6 Sep	West Point	College Football *Army vs. Marshall*
7 Sep	New York	USTA United States Open Women's Final
11 Sep	Nashville	College Football *Vanderbilt vs. Alabama*
12 Sep	Rochester	Lumberjack Contest Harness Racing

Date	City	Activity
13 Sep	Dover	Toured the outside of the Delaware State Capitol (due to construction)
13 Sep	Newark	College Football *Delaware vs. Villanova*
13 Sep	Atlantic City	Miss America Contest
14 Sep	Washington D.C.	NFL Jack Kent Cooke Stadium Dedication *Washington vs. Arizona*
15 Sep	Annapolis	Toured the Maryland State Capitol
15 Sep	Baltimore	MLB *Baltimore vs. Cleveland*
19 Sep	Washington D.C.	United States Davis Cup Tennis Tournament *USA vs. Australia*
20 Sep	Gainesville	College Football *Florida vs. Tennessee*
21 Sep	Tampa Bay	NFL *Tampa Bay vs. Miami*
22 Sep	Jacksonville	NFL *Jacksonville vs. Pittsburgh*
24 Sep	Montreal	MLB *Montreal vs. Florida*
25 Sep	Toronto	MLB *Toronto vs. Baltimore*

Date	City	Activity
26 Sep	Detroit	MLB *Detroit vs. New York (Yankees)*
27 Sep	Ann Arbor	College Football *Michigan vs. Notre Dame*
28 Sep	Pontiac	NFL *Detroit vs. Green Bay*
28 Sep	Minneapolis	NFL *Minnesota vs. Philadelphia*
29 Sep	Bismarck	Toured the North Dakota State Capitol
30 Sep	Pierre	Toured the South Dakota State Capitol

OCTOBER 1997

Date	City	Activity
1 Oct	Des Moines	Toured the Iowa State Capitol
2 Oct	Chicago	WPA World 9-Ball Pool Championship
3 Oct	Lincoln	College Volleyball *Nebraska vs. Iowa State*
4 Oct	Lincoln	College Football *Nebraska vs. Kansas State*
5 Oct	Green Bay	NFL *Green Bay vs. Tampa Bay*
9 Oct	Baltimore	MLB American League Playoff Game *Baltimore vs. Cleveland*

Date	City	Activity
11 Oct	New York	College Football *Columbia vs. Holy Cross*
11 Oct	New York	College Football *Fordham vs. Dartmouth*
12 Oct	New York	NFL *New York (Jets) vs. Miami*
13 Oct	Washington D.C.	NFL *Washington vs. Dallas*
14 Oct	Atlanta	MLB National League Championship *Atlanta vs. Florida*
16 Oct	Honolulu	Toured the Hawaii State Capitol
18 Oct	Kona	Ironman Triathlon Competition
22 Oct	Birmingham	Little League Football 5th & 6th Grade *Packers vs. Cowboys*
23 Oct	Cleveland	MLB World Series - Game 5 *Cleveland vs. Florida*
25 Oct	Miami	MLB World Series - Game 6 *Florida vs. Cleveland*
26 Oct	Miami	MLB World Series Championship Game - Game 7 *Florida vs. Cleveland*

Date	City	Activity
27 Oct	Charleston	Toured the West Virginia State Capitol
31 Oct	Boston	NBA *Boston vs. Chicago*

NOVEMBER 1997

Date	City	Activity
1 Nov	Boston	College Football *Boston College vs. Pittsburgh*
7 Nov	Raleigh	Toured the North Carolina State Capitol
8 Nov	State College	College Football *Penn State vs. Michigan*
9 Nov	Pittsburgh	PBA Tour Bowling Championships
9 Nov	Pittsburgh	NFL *Pittsburgh vs. Baltimore*
13 Nov	Baton Rouge	Toured the Louisiana State Capitol
13 Nov	Little Rock	Toured the Arkansas State Capitol
14 Nov	Austin	Toured the Texas State Capitol
15 Nov	Austin	College Football *Texas vs. Kansas*
15 Nov	Dallas	NBA *Dallas vs. Utah*
16 Nov	Dallas	NFL *Dallas vs. Washington*

Date	City	Activity
17 Nov	Jackson	Toured the Mississippi State Capitol
19 Nov	Hartford	ATP World Tennis Doubles Championships
20 Nov	Hartford	Toured the Connecticut State Capitol
20 Nov	Hartford	ATP World Tennis Doubles Championships
21 Nov	Storrs	College Field Hockey NCAA Semi-Finals *Princeton vs. North Carolina* *Virginia vs. Old Dominion*
21 Nov	Hartford	Women's College Basketball NIT Pre-Season Tournament *Connecticut vs. Nebraska*
21 Nov	Hartford	ATP World Tennis Doubles Championships
22 Nov	Hartford	ATP World Tennis Doubles Championships
27 Nov	San Juan	College Basketball Puerto Rican Shootout *Illinois vs. Wichita State* *Louisville vs. Hofstra* *Alabama vs. Georgia Tech*
29 Nov	Atlanta	College Football *Georgia Tech vs. Georgia*

Date	City	Activity

DECEMBER 1997

Date	City	Activity
2 Dec	Frankfort	Toured the Kentucky State Capitol
2 Dec	Chicago	College Basketball Big 8 Tournament *Arizona vs. Kansas*
3 Dec	Chicago	College Basketball Big 8 Tournament *North Carolina vs. Louisville* *Kentucky vs. Purdue*
6 Dec	New York	College Football *Army vs. Navy*
9 Dec	Birmingham	College Basketball *Alabama-Birmingham vs. Vanderbilt*
12 Dec	Carson City	Toured the Nevada State Capitol
14 Dec	Las Vegas	National Finals Rodeo
15 Dec	Phoenix	Toured the Arizona State Capitol
15 Dec	Santa Fe	Toured the New Mexico State Capitol
20 Dec	Birmingham	College Basketball Arby's Holiday Classic *Alabama vs. Tulane* *Alabama-Birmingham vs. Auburn*
23 Dec	Tallahassee	Toured the Florida State Capitol

Date	City	Activity
23 Dec	Tallahassee	College Basketball *Florida State vs. Arizona*
25 Dec	Montgomery	College Football Blue/Gray All-Star Game

Note: Part of my objective was to experience the flavor and atmosphere of the venues and people as much as the games themselves. Due to overlapping events, especially during regular season play, there were several occasions when I would only be able to see part of a game, and then I would have to leave to catch another game.